The Wrong Kind of Expert

Why Smart Investors Ignore Financial Advice and Think Like Business Owners

Ian Richards

THE WRONG KIND OF EXPERT

Published by: The Independent Investor

Cardiff • Wales

ISBN: 978-1-9194888-0-6

First Edition: 2026

printed in the region where ordered

Table of Contents

Introduction

You don't need to be the next Richard Branson or Mark Zuckerberg in order to generate wealth.

In fact, you don't even need to give up your job.

But if early retirement appeals to you, the advice you are going to receive in this book will certainly make that a possibility.

If the idea of becoming wealthy seems far-fetched, consider this: An 18-year-old starting their first job, saving just $20 per week invested in a simple stock index fund, will have amassed just over $1,000,000 by the time they reach the age of 66. By contributing to a tax-sheltered savings scheme (such as a ROTH in the USA or an ISA in the UK), this will provide a substantial income *completely free of tax*.

But I'm guessing that you don't want to wait that long. So we need to find a way to add a little juice to your returns.

Luckily, there is plenty of evidence to show how it can be done.

Consider the case of Anne Scheiber, a clerk who worked for the United States Internal Revenue Service. Although she never earned more than $4,000 per year throughout her life, she accumulated a fortune of $22 million. Her strategy? She simply invested in blue chip stocks like Coca-Cola, Pepsi and Bristol-Myers, reinvesting the dividends.

Of course, if it were that easy, I could end this book here. Coca-Cola and Pepsi are no longer the young 'growth engines' that they were when Anne Scheiber made her investments.

But there is no mystical art in finding the right investments.

Nearly all the world's best investors have been generous enough to share their insights and methods. And while no two investors are alike, two striking things stand out.

The first is that the methods they use are *completely contradictory* to the conventional advice given by most financial advisors today.

And the second is that they nearly all share certain key principles that are the foundation of their investing success.

In this book I present a clear and succinct distillation of the methods used by the most successful stock investors that have ever lived — a simple roadmap to investing success in the stock market.

Why Stocks?

The Power of Ownership

Before we dive into the methods of the great investors, we need to address a fundamental question: Why stocks?

The answer is simple. When you buy a stock, you become a part-owner of a real business. And throughout history, ownership of successful businesses has been the most reliable path to wealth.

Think about it. The wealthiest people in the world didn't get there by keeping money in a savings account or buying bonds. They built or owned businesses. Bill Gates owns Microsoft. Jeff Bezos owns Amazon. Warren Buffett owns Berkshire Hathaway.

When you buy stocks, you're doing exactly the same thing—you're buying ownership in businesses. You're just doing it in smaller pieces, and you're doing it through the stock market.

The Numbers Don't Lie

Let's look at what returns are possible with different approaches to investing.

$1,000 invested in Peter Lynch's Magellan fund in 1977 was worth over $27,000 just thirteen years later.

If you, or a parent, had invested $1,000 in Warren Buffett's Berkshire Hathaway when he took over in 1964, it would be worth around $12 million today.

These are extraordinary returns from stock investing. But what about other investment options?

Cash Savings: A bank deposit account today might pay 1.5% interest if you're lucky. At that rate, $1,000 grows to just $1,814 over forty years. Barely enough to keep pace with inflation.

Bonds: Government and corporate bonds might return 3-5% annually. Better than cash, but nowhere near the returns available from stocks. Warren Buffett himself has said that bonds "are among the most dangerous of assets" because inflation slowly destroys their purchasing power.

Real Estate: Property can produce good returns, but it requires enormous capital to get started, is highly illiquid (you can't sell half your house when you need cash), and comes with ongoing maintenance costs, property taxes, and the headache of being a landlord.

Stocks: The historical average annual return of the stock market is around 10%. But as we'll see throughout this book, by applying the methods of great investors, you can do significantly better.

Compound Magic

Here's where it gets interesting. Let's assume you're a 20-year-old with $1,000 to invest, and you want to know what it might be worth by the time you're 60.

At different rates of return, here's what happens:

Rate of Return	Value at Age 60
1.5% (cash)	$1,814
5% (bonds)	$7,040
10% (market average)	$45,259
15% (skilled investor)	$267,864
20% (expert investor)	$1,469,772

Look at that table carefully. The difference between 10% and 15%—just five percentage points—is the difference between $45,000 and $268,000.

The difference between 10% and 20% is the difference between having a nice nest egg and being a millionaire.

This is the magic of compound returns over time. Albert Einstein supposedly called compound interest "the eighth wonder of the world." He was right.

Grasping the significance of time and rate of return is the most important lesson you can learn from this book. Even a small increase in percentage returns can make a huge difference to an amount invested over time.

What About the Risk?

"But stocks are risky!" you might say. "I could lose everything!"

Let's address this head-on.

Yes, stocks can be volatile. In any given year, the stock market might be up 40% or down 40%. That volatility scares people. But here's what most people don't understand: over the long term, stocks are actually *less* risky than keeping your money in "safe" options like cash or bonds.

Why? Because of inflation.

If you keep $10,000 in a savings account paying 1.5% interest, and inflation runs at 3%, you're *losing* purchasing power every year. You might have more dollars, but each dollar buys less. Over forty years, inflation will destroy much of your wealth.

Stocks, on the other hand, represent ownership in real businesses that can raise their prices with inflation. They produce real goods and services that people need. They adapt and grow. Over long periods—and we're talking about investing for decades here, not months—stocks have consistently outperformed every other asset class.

The key is understanding what risk really means. Risk isn't volatility—the day-to-day ups and downs of stock prices. Risk is the permanent loss of capital. And the best way to avoid that is to invest in quality businesses and hold them for the long term.

As we'll see throughout this book, the great investors don't try to avoid volatility. They embrace it as an opportunity. When others are panicking and selling, they're buying. When others are euphoric and buying, they're patient or selling.

The Realistic Path

Now, I'm not suggesting that every reader of this book will achieve 20% annual returns. That would be unrealistic.

But here's what is realistic: By following the principles in this book, you should be able to beat the market average. If the market returns 10% and you return 12-15%, that difference compounds into enormous wealth over time.

And the beautiful thing about stock investing is that you don't need to start with a fortune. Anne Scheiber started with $5,000. You can start with even less. Many brokers now allow you to start investing with as little as $100.

The Plan

So here's the plan for this book:

We're going to learn from the best investors who have ever lived—people like Warren Buffett, Peter Lynch, and Philip Fisher. We're going to study how they think about businesses, how they value companies, and how they make investment decisions.

We're going to ignore conventional wisdom, because as we'll see, conventional wisdom is often wrong.

We're going to learn how to:

- Find great businesses worth owning
- Determine what they're really worth
- Buy them at the right price
- Hold them for the long term
- Know when to sell

Most importantly, we're going to develop the right temperament for investing—the ability to stay calm when others are panicking, and to act decisively when opportunity presents itself.

This isn't get-rich-quick. This is get-rich-surely.

Let's begin.

The Successful Investor's Portfolio

If you picked up this book expecting to learn the "secret formula" for stock picking, I have news for you: there is no secret formula.

But there is something better. There's a proven approach that the world's most successful investors use consistently. And it's completely different from what most financial advisors will tell you.

Conventional Wisdom vs. Reality

Most financial advisors will tell you that a balanced portfolio should be split between stocks and bonds. They'll say that stocks are "high risk" and bonds are "low risk." They'll advise that when you're young, you can afford more risk, so a high proportion of stocks is acceptable. But as you get older, the proportion that you invest in bonds should increase to protect your capital.

A common rule of thumb is to use your age as a percentage for bonds. So a 20-year-old should invest 20% in bonds, and a 50-year-old should invest 50% in bonds.

They'll also tell you to diversify broadly—to own hundreds or even thousands of stocks through index funds or mutual funds. And they'll tell you to "rebalance" your portfolio regularly, selling your winners to buy more of your losers.

All of this advice seems very sensible. No advisor is ever going to run into trouble by advising you to invest this way. And if the height of your ambition is to just beat inflation and return a little below the market average—along the lines of 8% per year—then if you follow this advice you will do just fine.

But if you want to build real wealth —join that small handful of investors who have accumulated millions from modest stakes—then you will need to think again.

How the Best Investors Actually Invest

The way that successful investors manage their money is completely different.

In Guy Thomas's book 'Free Capital', Thomas interviews a dozen highly successful UK investors, half of whom have accumulated over £1 million tax-free in ISA accounts. Investor 'Vernon' started investing in 1998 and became an ISA millionaire by 2005—an incredibly impressive performance when you consider that over this period the maximum annual limit for investing in an ISA was just £7,000 per year.

Vernon summed up his attitude to convention neatly: "Learning modern portfolio theory to pick investments is like learning physics to play snooker."

In researching this book, I have surveyed the methods of a wide range of investors, including Shelby Davis, Peter Lynch, Warren Buffett, Philip Fisher, Tom Gayner, Benjamin Graham, and many others. None of these, or any of the twelve investors in Thomas's book, use an approach anywhere near the conventional approach.

Just as snooker players ignore physics and concentrate on making the shot in front of them, successful investors focus on businesses. To become a top-level snooker player, having an aptitude for the game takes second place to being able to remain cool under pressure. And for investors, a cool temperament is far more important than a facility in selecting securities.

The Bond Fallacy

Let's address bonds first.

According to Vanguard, the historical average annual return of a 100% bond portfolio is 5.5%. The historical average annual return of a 100% stock portfolio is 10.2%.

If you are investing for the long term, one would ask the question: Why should I hamstring my returns by adding bonds to the portfolio?

Bonds appear safe because they offer a fixed rate of return, together with the assumption that the capital value of a bond is assured. But as interest rates vary, so does the capital value of bonds. Any notion of capital protection is illusory.

Referring to bonds in his 2012 letter to shareholders, Warren Buffett said: "They are among the most dangerous of assets. Over the past century these instruments have destroyed the purchasing power of investors in many countries, even as these holders continued to receive timely payments of interest and principal."

Very few successful investors hold bonds in their portfolio. The clear implication is that to make superior investment returns, bonds should be avoided.

This book is about stock investing, and from this point forward, we will focus exclusively on stocks.

Diversification: How Much Is Enough?

Your attention may be drawn to the portfolios of two of the world's greatest investors. Peter Lynch held 1,400 stocks in his Magellan portfolio. Shelby Davis held over 1,200 stocks at the time of his death.

So should you own thousands of stocks?

No.

For an investor with modest goals who makes a small monthly contribution into index funds, spreading the risk over many stocks makes perfect sense. But if you're looking to make superior returns, a more focused approach is required.

Although Davis and Lynch appeared to favor portfolios with a large number of stocks, a more detailed look at their habits reveals a different picture.

Shelby Davis may have had over 1,200 stocks when he finished, but that was not how he made the bulk of his fortune. With $50,000 cash, he started in 1948 with a portfolio of seven insurance stocks. By the mid-1950s he had rotated into 32 long-term insurance holdings. For the vast majority of his investing career, Davis's portfolio contained 30 to 50 stocks.

Peter Lynch's fund held 1,400 stocks, but that didn't reflect his personal approach to investing. He explained it like this: "A foolish diversity is the hobgoblin of small investors... I'd be comfortable owning between three and ten stocks."

He also added, "Although I own 1,400 stocks in all, half of my fund's assets are invested in 100 stocks and two-thirds in 200 stocks." The smallest 500 companies made up just 1% of his fund.

On leaving Magellan and becoming responsible for his personal investments, Lynch wrote, "You may be wondering what's happened to my investing habits since I left Magellan. Instead of following thousands of companies, now I follow maybe fifty."

Tom Gayner, the highly respected investment manager at Markel, holds a portfolio of just over 100 stocks, but 74% of the amount invested is in just 30.

Of the twelve successful investors studied by Guy Thomas, nine had portfolios of fewer than fifty investments, and of those nine, six had portfolios of fewer than ten investments.

Warren Buffett has 47 stocks in the Berkshire Hathaway portfolio. For a portfolio of $108 billion, that's not a huge number!

The conclusion is clear: most highly successful investors have concentrated portfolios. A portfolio size of around fifteen to twenty stocks would be appropriate for most investors. A portfolio of six stocks would seem to be the lowest reasonable limit if you prefer concentration. A maximum portfolio size of around fifty stocks would be an appropriate upper limit if you have the time and inclination to understand that number of businesses.

Where Do the Returns Come From?

Here's something crucial to understand: In a diversified portfolio, most of your returns will come from a small number of stocks.

Peter Lynch remarks, "All you need for a lifetime of successful investing is a few big winners, and the pluses from those will overwhelm the minuses from the stocks that don't work out."

Warren Buffett's mentor, Benjamin Graham, was persuaded by his business partner to make a 50% investment in the insurance company GEICO. This one stock returned 562 times the investment (from 1948 to 1972)—a bigger gain than that returned by all of the firm's other investments combined.

A glance at the returns for The Motley Fool's investor services reveals that while both services beat the market, most of the returns derive from a small handful out of hundreds of stock selections.

Shelby Davis made his initial fortune from just a small handful of insurance stocks.

This is not a phenomenon confined to individual investors. In 2014, 55% of the returns of the S&P 500 index came from just 36 out of 500 stocks. And 20% of the returns came from just five stocks.

When you construct a portfolio of stocks, it may be evenly balanced initially, but over time a small number of stocks will outperform and begin to dominate the portfolio.

The way you handle this will be crucial to your long-term success. If you follow conventional advice and rebalance regularly, you will be "cutting the flowers to water the weeds."

When the right opportunity arises, successful investors are prepared to commit a huge percentage of their portfolio to a stock in which they have high conviction.

Back in 1963, American Express was embroiled in a major financial scandal and the share price collapsed from $65 to $37. After carrying out careful research, Warren Buffett became convinced that the company was fundamentally sound and invested 40% of his fund in the company. The subsequent rebound in the stock was one of the main catalysts that set Buffett on his way to becoming the world's greatest investor.

While great investors do not appear keen to keep huge bets (50%+) allocated to a single stock for extended periods, they are content to allocate a significant percentage of their portfolio to high-quality businesses indefinitely. As of March 2016, Buffett's Berkshire Hathaway had 21% of its equity portfolio invested in Kraft-Heinz, 18% invested in Wells Fargo, and 14% invested in Coca-Cola.

If you can recognize quality businesses and have the temperament to hold them through thick and thin, then you have found the secret to great investing.

Investing Style: Buy and Hold

There are two types of participants in the stock market: Traders and Investors.

Some participants advocate a "cut and thrust" investment style—jumping in and out of investments at opportune moments. Players who trade over very short time frames are known as "Day Traders."

On the other hand, Warren Buffett, Peter Lynch, and Shelby Davis are known as "Long-Term Buy and Hold" investors—often abbreviated as LTBH investors.

Which style produces the best results?

In August 2013, The Wall Street Journal stated: "The three top spots in the Hulbert Financial Digest's five-year rankings through June 30 of more than 200 investment-advisory services all buy and hold quality companies."

Many would regard Warren Buffett—the epitome of buy-and-hold investing—as the most successful investor of all time. Buffett says that his favorite holding period is "forever."

Peter Lynch writes, "The typical winner in the Lynch portfolio generally takes three to ten years or more to play out."

Of the dozen investors surveyed in 'Free Capital', six invested for the long term, five for the medium term, and only one was a day trader. After three years, the author contacted the twelve investors to enquire about their performance. Most continued to perform well, but the lone day trader had lost to the market.

It is fair to conclude that your most likely recipe for success is to follow a buy-and-hold strategy.

But there is a caveat. Despite advocating holding "forever" as a strategy, Buffett will often sell stocks and rotate his holdings. Lynch likes to switch in and out of positions in slow-growing companies. Shelby Davis was renowned as a long-term holder, but by the mid-50s all the names in his original portfolio were gone. He had moved on to a new set of companies that he felt comfortable holding for extended periods.

In summary: you should buy great companies and hold them for long periods—but don't be afraid to sell when the need arises.

The Magic Plan

In the previous chapters, we looked at the magic of compounding and discovered that the best way to get a high rate of return is to have a relatively concentrated portfolio consisting entirely of stocks.

By following and adapting the methods of the great investors, the vast majority of people are quite capable of amassing well over a million over a lifetime. There is a simple and effective plan:

The Magic Plan:

- **Don't get into debt**—especially credit card debt.
- **Follow Buffett's advice:** "Do not save what is left after spending, but spend what is left after saving."
- **Keep an Emergency Fund** - this book is about money that you can afford to set aside over the long term.
- **Build an investment portfolio** by creating a collection of stocks—preferably in a tax-sheltered account.
- **Start simple.** Begin with index funds if you're just starting out, then transition to individual stocks as your knowledge grows.
- **Keep learning.** The more you understand about businesses and investing, the better your returns will be.

The first two steps are self-explanatory, but the rest merit further comment.

Starting Your Journey

When you first start investing, you have a choice. You can dive straight into individual stocks, or you can start with index funds and gradually transition to individual stocks as your knowledge and confidence grow.

There's no right or wrong answer here—it depends on your personality and circumstances.

The index fund approach is safer and simpler. You can start investing immediately without needing to analyze individual companies. You'll get market returns, which as we've seen, will make you wealthy over time. As you read this book and learn more about individual companies, you can gradually add individual stocks to your portfolio.

The individual stock approach offers higher potential returns but requires more work and knowledge. If you're eager to get started and willing to put in the time to learn, there's no reason you can't start with individual stocks right away. Many investors use a hybrid approach: They keep a core holding in index funds while building a portfolio of individual stocks on the side.

How Much Do You Need to Start?

Here's the good news: You don't need much.

Many brokers now allow you to start investing with as little as $100. Some even allow fractional share purchases, meaning you can buy a portion of an expensive stock like Amazon or Berkshire Hathaway.

However, you should be aware of trading costs. A good rule of thumb is not to purchase stock if the dealing fees amount to more than 2%. For example, if your broker charges $10 per trade, then a single trade should be a minimum of $500. One of the best advances of recent years is that trading costs have dropped dramatically, making it much easier for small investors to buy individual stocks.

The Learning Portfolio

If you're transitioning from index funds to individual stocks, or if you're just starting out, consider creating a "learning portfolio."

Here's how it might work:

Conservative approach: Wait until you have $10,000. Keep $5,000 in index funds and start a learning portfolio of five individual stocks at $1,000 each.

Moderate approach: Start with $5,000. Create a portfolio of five to ten individual stocks.

Aggressive approach: Start with $2,000. Create a portfolio of four to five individual stocks.

The key is to start with an amount you're comfortable losing while you learn. Because let's be honest: you will make mistakes. Every investor does. The goal is to make small mistakes while you're learning, not large ones.

Is It Worth the Effort?

At this point, you may be wondering if it's all worthwhile — shouldn't you just stick to index funds?

Let's look at the numbers.

An index fund returning 10% over 40 years turns $1,000 into $45,259.

An investor making just 5% more — 15% annually — gets $267,864.

Is that worth the effort? Only you can answer that. But consider this: the knowledge and skills you develop by learning to invest in individual stocks will benefit you for the rest of your life. You'll understand how businesses work. You'll be able to spot opportunities. You'll develop patience and emotional discipline. These are valuable skills that extend far beyond just making money.

Can You Really Beat the Professionals?

You may be wondering if it's really feasible that you can beat the professionals and beat the market.

The answer is an emphatic yes.

Peter Lynch says that the average investor should be able to beat the market by two to five percent through investing in individual stocks. And as Guy Thomas's book testifies, many individual investors do considerably better than that. (From personal experience I can tell you that since I sold my business in 2013, by following the approach taken in this book, I have crushed the market with returns averaging over 35% per year.)

With a little discipline and application, there is no reason why you shouldn't achieve a fifteen percent return over the long term. At this rate, even if you didn't start saving until the age of forty, by saving $5,000 per year you would achieve returns of over $1 million by age sixty-five.

You have several advantages over professional investors:

Time horizon: You can hold stocks forever if you want. Professional fund managers are judged quarterly and face pressure to show constant results.

Flexibility: You can invest in any company, no matter how small. Large funds can only invest in large companies—they're too big to take meaningful positions in small, fast-growing companies.

No career risk: If you make a mistake, you won't lose your job. This allows you to think independently and make contrarian bets that professionals can't.

Personal knowledge: You see products and services in your daily life that Wall Street analysts might miss. This is a huge advantage that Peter Lynch exploited throughout his career.

Now that we have a plan, we need to consider how we will find these winning investments. But before we can find them, we need to understand what we're looking for.

And that starts with understanding what a stock really is.

Stocks Are Businesses

The Most Important Lesson

If you take away only one idea from this book, let it be this:

A stock is not a lottery ticket. It's ownership in a real business.

How Most People Think About Stocks

Every day the stocks jostle with each other as their prices go up and down. Picking the stocks that will go up seems just like going to the races and picking the winning horse.

Each stock has a ticker symbol, such as AAPL, FB, or MCD (Apple, Facebook, McDonald's). The similarity with lottery tickets strengthens—the ticker symbols are like ticket numbers. Feel like a gamble? Let's try to pick the winning ticker!

Some traders favor a stock with a price chart that is going up. They assume that the trend will continue. Others are drawn to a stock that has been in decline. It must be due for a turnaround!

If you treat the stock market like a lottery, you may have some fun. But your chances of long-term financial success are pretty close to zero.

How Great Investors Think About Stocks

The most successful investors have an entirely different outlook.

Peter Lynch sums it up nicely: "Invest in companies, not in the stock market."

Warren Buffett puts it like this: "Your goal as an investor should simply be to purchase, at a rational price, a part interest in an easily understandable business."

When Shelby Davis worked for the New York State insurance department, he became intimately involved with the financial details of many insurance companies. It was his knowledge of the *business* that enabled him to identify undervalued companies and gave him his edge.

All of the great long-term investors have a "business first" approach.

Thinking Like a Business Owner

Many of us, if we had the chance, would be quite happy to own a share in a thriving local business—maybe a busy restaurant, hair salon, or automotive service center. If you held a 50% stake in such a business, how would you look after your investment?

Perhaps you might check on the accounts every six months. It would be wise to pop in every now and then to make sure that trade was brisk and that the customers were happy.

Would you be constantly checking to find out the current resale value? Not likely. If you did, and you found that you could have purchased your 50% stake slightly cheaper, would you be tempted to sell out immediately in case the value of your half of the business declined further? Almost certainly not. As long as the business was doing well and profits were rolling in, you would be quite content to remain a part-owner for the long term.

A business with thriving trade and good profits will surely be worth considerably more in a few years' time, irrespective of any day-to-day fluctuations in market value.

Ownership of a stock in a publicly quoted company is no different in principle from part ownership in a local business.

The only major difference—and it is a significant difference—is that the price of the stock in the public company is published every day for the whole world to see. And the price may fluctuate wildly in response to interest rates, political uncertainty, the performance of the Chinese economy—or any number of other things that are highly unlikely to have any bearing on the long-term performance of the business.

Given access to this information, investors are liable to react emotionally and decide to sell out or trade their stake for another stock, which in turn will have its own gyrations and produce further anguish.

The successful investor learns to tune out this "noise" and is content to focus solely on the performance of the business, holding for the long term and deciding to sell only if there is a genuine change in the business itself.

Your Journey Begins

Now that you understand what stocks really are—ownership stakes in real businesses—we're ready to begin learning how to evaluate those businesses.

In the next chapter, we'll look at what makes a great business worth owning. We'll develop a checklist of qualities to look for, drawn from the methods of the world's most successful investors.

This is where investing gets interesting. This is where you'll develop the skills that will serve you for a lifetime.

Evaluating a Company for Investment

Introduction

If investing in great businesses is the key to successful investment, it follows that the ability to select businesses that will outperform their peers is the most important skill that an investor must develop.

Even great investors have found that this skill does not develop overnight. Over the years, Warren Buffett has changed his mind considerably about the type of company in which he wishes to invest. In his early years, he focused on companies holding assets with values that were not fairly reflected on the balance sheet—such as railroad companies with large property portfolios. Property is often shown on the accounts at the original cost, but its present-day market value may have increased considerably.

As Buffett developed his investing expertise, with the help and influence of his business partner Charlie Munger, he began to focus on businesses with great revenue-producing potential. He gravitated toward companies with great brands that could continue to generate revenue for years to come, such as See's Candy or American Express.

In 'Free Capital', Guy Thomas notes that all of the investors studied had an initial period of poor performance before they developed their skill and became successful investors. To become a great investor, you will need to be patient and persistent in developing the ability to recognize superior businesses.

The main difficulty in seeing success stories before they occur is that there is no single metric that can be used to identify a great business. The uninitiated often believe that great investors are great number crunchers, identifying investments through superior analytical skill.

But it is often not just the numbers that tell the full story. Management quality, culture, and the company's ability to innovate and judge the market can all be just as important. It is this combination of the qualitative with the quantitative that makes investing such an interesting and rewarding endeavor.

You don't need to have a high level of numerical skill to become a great investor. Thomas notes of his dozen investors, "None of the investors relies on modern portfolio theory... or indeed on any sophisticated quantitative analysis... despite the fact that several... have strong quantitative or business school backgrounds." Charlie Munger said of Buffett, "Warren often talks about these discounted cash flows, but I've never seen him do one."

A dislike for complication is a common quality of high performers. Between 1973 and 1998, John Malone returned a staggering 30.3 percent annually to his shareholders, but he never used spreadsheets, preferring to assess projects using simple calculations. William Thorndike writes of Malone in 'The Outsiders': "He quickly developed a simple rule that became the cornerstone of the company's acquisition program... This analysis could be done on a single sheet of paper (or if necessary, the back of a napkin)."

In 'One Up on Wall Street', Peter Lynch describes the various parameters he looks for in order to evaluate a business. Shunning sophisticated analysis, he states, "I ignore short-term debt in my calculations. The purists can fret all they want about this, but why complicate matters unnecessarily?"

But don't take this as a sign of carelessness in his investigation. Lynch is diligent in studying a number of indicators. But his assessment methods are very straightforward, requiring only basic arithmetic. Is cash growing? What is the ratio of share price to earnings? And how does this compare to earnings growth?

All great investors are able to determine whether a business has strong finances using only basic mathematics combined with a little common sense. In fact, it would seem that skilled investors shy away from complex calculations, as they often offer a misleading precision. A common-sense "feel" for numbers is the most important aptitude that you need to develop in order to make a realistic assessment of how a business is performing.

It is evident, then, that to be a great investor you do not need superior analytical skill. Perhaps more surprisingly, many investors contend that no more than limited intelligence is required. Buffett said, "Success in investing doesn't correlate with I.Q.. Once you have ordinary intelligence, what you need is the temperament to control the urges that get other people into trouble in investing."

Stocks may appreciate by 10% a year over the long term. But in a single year they may be up 40% — or more. Or they may be down 40% — or more. The best investors neither break out the champagne nor look for the nearest balcony. They simply keep their cool and focus on the performance of each individual company as a business.

This is good news for most of us. God-given gifts of intelligence or superior mathematical ability are not required in order to invest successfully. Learning to control our emotions holds the key.

In order to beat the market, we have to find stocks that the market has undervalued.

A company's valuation depends on two things:

> First, an arithmetic valuation derived from a company's earnings, balance sheet, and current market multiples. (And if you do not know what I mean by multiples — don't fret, we will cover this in detail later.)
>
> Second, a qualitative evaluation of a company's ability to innovate or differentiate itself from its peers.

There is no shortage of spreadsheets and databases on Wall Street — so it is likely that most companies with strong prima facie figures have already been assigned a healthy valuation by "The Street."

The best hope for the individual investor is to look beyond the raw numbers. You need to find the businesses with hidden attributes that the "spreadsheet jockeys" have missed.

Combine these with strong financial fundamentals, and you have a great chance of finding a winning investment.

Attributes of a Successful Business

The factors that most successful investors look for in a business are:

- Competitive Advantage
- Good Management
- Strong Balance Sheet
- Growing Revenues
- Growing Profitability
- Strong Cash Flow
- Good Return on Capital
- Strong Corporate Culture
- Total Addressable Market
- Reinvestment Potential
- Low Capital Requirement
- Personal Experience
- Low Profile
- Special Circumstances
- Reasonable Share Price

We will look at each of these areas in turn.

Competitive Advantage

A company's competitive advantage derives from an attribute or collection of attributes that enable it to achieve superior performance relative to its peers.

There are a number of different ways in which a company can achieve a competitive advantage.

The most spectacular competitive advantage belongs to the company that can turn a market upside down by providing a totally new product that renders its competitors obsolete (think digital cameras vs. photographic film, calculators vs. slide rules, or temporary storage in the computer industry where floppy disks were supplanted by CDs which were supplanted by memory sticks which were supplanted by online storage).

On the other hand, a company can achieve dominance in an industry simply by doing things better than its competitors. Costco didn't invent retail, but a fastidious attention to detail has made it one of the most respected companies in the industry. Investors holding the stock in 2009 will have more than trebled their money over the succeeding six years, for a return of around 23% annually.

A company that can dominate an industry through holding a rock-solid patent in an emerging technology will be able to sustain a competitive advantage more easily than a company that has to knock it out of the park with strong execution year in, year out.

In order to evaluate how a company derives its competitive advantage, it can be helpful to place the company in a suitable category:

- Disruptive Innovators
- Sustaining Innovators
- Financial Engineers
- Brilliant Executors
- IP Kings

Some companies may fit more than one category.

Let's take each one in turn.

Disruptive Innovators

Disruptive innovators derive their advantage by completely changing an industry, often rendering competitive firms or products obsolete by introducing a new and better way of doing things. The classic analysis and description of disruptive innovation can be found in Clayton Christensen's book, 'The Innovator's Dilemma'.

Christensen shows how young, growing companies with disruptive products can beat established market leaders — often with fatal consequences for the former champion.

By taking a detailed look at a number of disparate industries, such as disk drives, mechanical excavators, and steel making, he shows how the entrenched players were unable to react to the disruptive innovator until it was too late.

Seagate was the dominant player in the market for disk drives for desktop computers. Seagate's drives were 5.25" in diameter. When Conner introduced a new 3.5" format drive, Seagate was unfazed. Their customers were not asking for a new size; they wanted more capacity. Seagate's engineers were actively engaged in producing a 3.5" drive, but when Seagate found no enthusiasm for the drive from their customers, they decided to shut down the project.

Conner's smaller, lighter 3.5" drive may not have had the capacity of Seagate's drives, but it had key advantages in the burgeoning market for portable computers. With orders from Compaq Computer, Conner had the resources to improve the speed and capacity of its drives. Eventually everyone recognized the advantages of the 3.5" drive, and Conner displaced Seagate as the dominant supplier of disk drives in the market for both portable and desktop computers.

Conner was the disruptive innovator.

Ironically, in an earlier period when the 5.25" drive was first introduced, it was Seagate that was the disruptor. Seagate displaced the manufacturers that produced the 8" drives originally used in mini-computers.

Being a disruptor offers no protection against being disrupted.

Another classic example of disruptive innovation is the Kodak company. Kodak led the photography industry for many years but then succumbed to bankruptcy when digital cameras replaced the need for photographic film.

Sustaining Innovators

Sustaining innovators take an existing technology and keep developing it to produce better and better performance.

In the market for 5.25" disk drives, Seagate was a sustaining innovator—maintaining their dominance by continuously improving their drives.

Apple didn't invent the personal computer, digital music player, or mobile phone. But it has produced products in all three categories that are arguably better than those produced by Apple's competitors.

Apple is brilliant at taking an existing product and constantly refining it until it reaches its full potential. The company has established a solid reputation for elegant design and high quality. Customers are prepared to pay high prices for Apple's products. Although Apple does not sell as many phones as its competitors, it makes far greater profits. Apple's pricing power enables it to sell products with much higher margins than its rivals.

Apple is the epitome of a successful sustaining innovator. The danger for Apple is that it relies heavily on sales of mobile phones. If a disruptive innovator arrives on the scene with a product that can replace the mobile phone, Apple could be in trouble.

In the automobile industry, cars have been using the internal combustion engine (ICE) for well over a hundred years. Over this time, companies such as BMW have been refining the product to produce levels of performance and efficiency that would have seemed fantastic to the original engineers. BMW is another great example of a sustaining innovator.

Tesla produces cars that are powered by electricity. The engine has been replaced by a battery. The complex, highly developed ICE with over two thousand moving parts has been replaced by a simple electric motor with fewer than twenty moving parts.

Tesla is a disruptive innovator.

Now most car companies are producing electric cars, and many Chinese companies are starting to produce efficient, competitive models, but they are finding it difficult to produce them as profitably as Tesla.

Meanwhile, Tesla is now concentrating on self-driving cars and humanoid robots, starting a new wave of disruption. Christensen contends that it is very difficult for an incumbent company to survive a challenge from a disruptive upstart. It will be interesting to see what happens.

Financial Engineers

It may seem natural to assume that great business leaders are masters of corporate management. They build efficient operations based on modern computer systems. They know how to motivate managers and staff. And they have a superior understanding of their products and how they fit into the market.

Surprisingly, an analysis of the businesses that have produced the best returns for their shareholders shows that the best CEOs are not these types of people at all. To be sure—the skills mentioned above are all necessary to run a business. But great leaders delegate these tasks to great operational managers. The best CEOs rise above the humdrum day-to-day concerns of management and instead focus on **capital allocation**.

When Tom Murphy was running Capital Cities, producing a staggering *average* annual return of *twenty percent* over *twenty-nine years*, he focused almost all of his energy on capital allocation. His colleague, Dan Burke, was given free rein to run the business as efficiently as possible. Burke's job was generating the cash. Murphy would decide what to do with it.

There is no special mystique surrounding the techniques used by great capital allocators. When shares are cheap—they buy them back. When shares are expensive—they use them for acquisitions. When debt is cheap—they borrow for expansion or acquisition.

Techniques which are directed toward the use of capital rather than toward the operational side of the business are commonly referred to as **financial engineering**.

Great capital allocators have three essential qualities:

- Patience
- The ability to spot an opportunity and seize it
- Adaptability

If necessary, the best capital harvesters will bide their time for years while they wait for an opportunity to arise. When the opportunity comes, they strike quickly. They adapt their actions to the circumstances. At one time they may be acquiring businesses. At another they may be disposing of them.

In short, they do whatever is necessary in order to achieve the highest possible return on their capital at any given time.

All this may seem like common sense, but very few CEOs possess the discipline to manage capital effectively. Most CEOs think like operational managers. On the occasions when they do make a capital decision — such as to buy back shares — they are likely to do it for the wrong reason, and often at the wrong time. A common reason for buying back shares is to reverse the effect of using stock to pay employees (usually referred to as **stock-based compensation**) — a decision made to a fixed timetable, regardless of whether the stock is trading at an attractive price or not.

Many successful companies with household names achieved their success despite being poor capital allocators. Perhaps it is too much to ask that a company should have a CEO who is both a creative innovator and a great capital allocator?

For the best example of the power of capital allocation, there is no better place to turn than to the master himself, Warren Buffett.

Berkshire Hathaway may be a trillion-dollar company, but until he retired in January 2026 Buffett ran it from an office in Omaha with just twenty-five staff. Each business unit is totally independent. Buffett sat at the center, perusing the brief summaries of operational performance sent in regularly by his managers. Any surplus cash generated by the various business units was remitted to Berkshire. Buffett's job? Allocating the capital in the most efficient way.

It will be interesting to see how Greg Abel carries the mantle of the great man.

Using this simple model, Buffett has become a legend. "Knocking it out of the park" doesn't even begin to describe the performance of Berkshire Hathaway's stock, which has outperformed the S&P by a *hundredfold.*

Often these days, financial engineering is referred to rather condescendingly. If a company has just raised its earnings per share by buying back stock, a commentator may say, "Well, they raised their EPS, but that was just financial engineering," as if to say, "OK—but the business hasn't performed any better, so that doesn't justify an increase in the share price."

Like most daft statements, this can be countered by a reductio ad absurdum. If the 1.6 billion shares in Walt Disney were reduced to one, would that share be worth any more than it was before the reduction? Answer — of course it would, as it now represents the value of the entire business (in fact, it would be worth 1.6 billion times as much). Increasing the EPS by reducing the share count is not "just financial engineering"; it's a valid way to permanently increase the value of each share.

If you are tempted to downplay a company's worth because it has been ascribed to "financial engineering," simply remember this: the companies that have produced the best returns for shareholders have all been run by great capital allocators.

Brilliant Executors

Some companies excel simply by being good at what they do.

Take Starbucks, for example. There is no impediment stopping any competitor from setting up a coffee chain to rival Starbucks. In fact, Starbucks's success has attracted a whole host of new entrants to that market.

But through simply being a great executor, Howard Schultz propelled Starbucks to be the leader of the pack. As the company's brand and reputation has grown, it has become more and more difficult for new entrants to mount a successful challenge.

Another great example of execution is Costco.

Jim Sinegal believes in an ethical approach to business. He built trust from his customers, nurtured his staff, and treated his suppliers fairly. Founding Costco in 1983 with fellow entrepreneur Jeffrey Brotman, he paired this stakeholder-friendly approach with a lean business model and a laser focus on low prices. By sticking fastidiously to this approach, he took Costco from nothing to be the second-largest retailer in the world in 2015.

Costco's decision to give priority to other stakeholders over shareholders has not always resonated well with Wall Street. But early shareholders who recognized Sinegal's dedication and ability to execute have been far more richly rewarded than those who were tempted to seek the short-term quick buck on offer elsewhere.

IP Kings

IP is a commonly used abbreviation for Intellectual Property, such as copyright in a software product, a trade secret, or a patent for an industrial process.

A great way to secure long-term returns is to invent something useful and then sit back and collect royalties.

IP-based companies will often invest heavily to create some kind of intellectual property that they can then exploit at high margins for many years to come.

A software company may spend years creating a product, but once it exists, the product can be sold for a high price with minimal cost of sale. Microsoft is a great example. It invested heavily over the years producing MS-DOS, Windows, and Microsoft Office. Once created, all of these products became huge cash cows for the company and continue to do so to the present.

In the computer industry, microprocessor companies like Qualcomm and ARM Holdings are able to license their designs to other companies and collect a steady stream of royalties with no ongoing costs.

Companies like Facebook and LinkedIn have to invest heavily in building a platform to host billions of users—but once the platform is built, they can grow revenues for years with little additional capital cost for infrastructure.

One danger to be aware of with IP-centered companies is that their product may be displaced by a new technology. This is a particular danger with patents, which have a relatively short term before expiry. Businesses that invest heavily in research and development (**R&D**) may be able to protect against obsolescence by creating new IP to replace the old. But there is always a danger that a disruptive innovator will supplant their IP and render it worthless.

Any business that is "capital light" has great potential to be highly profitable — and the IP kings are the most profitable of them all.

Summary

A sustainable competitive advantage is the most important quality that you should look for in a business in order to achieve superior investment returns.

Let's look at some of the remaining key qualities associated with successful companies.

Management

A company's success will depend to a large extent on the quality of the management team, and more particularly, on the quality of the chief executive.

Just look at some of the greatest success stories in business—General Electric, Microsoft, Virgin, Amazon, Dell, Facebook. The company's greatest periods of success coincided with the tenure of great leaders: Jack Welch, Bill Gates, Richard Branson, Jeff Bezos, Michael Dell, and Mark Zuckerberg.

Some great companies have come upon hard times following a change at the top. John Sculley was hired to take Apple to the next level, but the marketing-oriented approach which had served him so well at Pepsi Cola did not translate to a technology-centered business like Apple. His decision to effectively fire Steve Jobs was disastrous, and Apple did not recover until Sculley was gone and Jobs was once more at the helm.

Recognizing the importance of great management is one thing. But can we pin down those qualities that make the best managers?

Some great managers are autocratic, while others like to build upon consensus. Some great managers focus on technology. Others see the customer as their main priority. Many great businesses owe their success to an empowered, committed workforce where managers place a high premium on employee welfare. Other successful businesses operate on a "hire and fire" basis where low-paid staff are motivated by a fear of redundancy.

Costco and Amazon are both great success stories in modern retailing, but the management styles of Jim Sinegal and Jeff Bezos couldn't be more different.

In truth, the only way to identify a great manager is to judge them by results. It was not through mean-spiritedness that Jobs was kept from the CEO job at Apple. His odd habits and maniacal focus on detail were sure signs to most observers that he would be a disaster as a CEO. But as it turned out, Apple's great success was not in spite of Jobs's leadership; it was because of it.

So from the quiet Henry Singleton at Teledyne to the larger than life style of Elon Musk at Tesla and SpaceX, there is only one thing that distinguishes outstanding management — outstanding results.

In assessing a company's management, therefore, the first thing to look at is track record. What has the CEO achieved? Prior to the current appointment, does the CEO have a long record of success? Has this success been achieved in related industries?

The CEO's outlook and point of view is also an important factor. Not because it will affect the performance of the business, but because it may affect how you feel about the investment. We will look at how you can develop an investment style in chapter twelve. But for now, it is enough to say that it will be difficult for you to support an investment in a business if your own point of view conflicts markedly with the business philosophy of the CEO. (And it is the business philosophy that matters - politics are a different thing).

Management is a prime consideration in evaluating an investment, but as Buffett once said, "When a management with a reputation for brilliance tackles a business with a reputation for bad economics, it is the reputation of the business that remains intact."

Let's move on to look at the other key qualities that you should look for in a business.

Strong Balance Sheet

Even the best businesses will have unexpected problems and issues. When these occur, it is important that the business has sufficient resources to weather the storm and meet its commitments without difficulty.

The financial strength of a business is depicted on its **balance sheet**. The balance sheet comes in two parts.

The first part lists the assets of the business: cash, property, goods held in stock, amounts owed by customers, and other items that may be regarded as assets (more on this later).

The second part of the balance sheet lists the liabilities of the business: overdrafts, loans, amounts owed to suppliers, and any other liabilities.

The difference between assets and liabilities represents the total profits made by the business from inception to the present. This profit is attributable to the business's owners, so in that respect it is also a liability, and is shown on the balance sheet as shareholders' equity. It follows that the liabilities section of the balance sheet must always add up to the same total as the assets section—therefore it balances—hence the name "balance sheet."

If the liabilities add up to more than the assets, the business owners' equity is negative (i.e., the owners "owe" money to the business in order to make it good), and the business is insolvent.

A business with lots of cash and a low figure for liabilities is said to have a strong balance sheet. A business like this is in a strong position to weather short-term problems.

A business with only just enough cash to cover liabilities will have problems making its payments in the event of hard times, and this makes the business a risky investment.

Lack of cash is not always a bad sign—businesses with strong growth prospects and reliable sources of cash flow may need to borrow to maximize their growth potential.

But a precarious cash position should be seen at the very least as a major red flag. We will look at balance sheets and how we can interpret them later in this chapter.

Growing Revenues

The balance sheet of a business represents a snapshot in time.

It depicts the assets and liabilities of the business as they were on the date that the balance sheet was produced. Investors are more interested in the future than the present. Or as Markel's Tom Gayner puts it, he likes to look at a business as if it were a movie, not a snapshot.

At the outset of the digital revolution in cameras, a business selling photographic film may have had a strong balance sheet. But what about its prospects?

It is not cash in the bank today that is so important as being able to see a continuous stream of growing future receipts.

The **revenue** of a business is the total amount of sales that the business makes. This is sometimes also referred to as **turnover** (UK).

If we see a business that has been growing revenue steadily, it gives confidence that the management can execute well, and as long as there are no other factors to the contrary, we can assume that the business has a good chance to grow revenues further in the future.

Growing Profitability

Revenue is important, but revenue that does not lead to profit is worth nothing.

A business may sell a lot of product by pricing it at a low mark-up—showing growing revenues but no corresponding growth in profit.

Good businesses can demand higher prices, and hence enjoy higher mark-ups, which means that growing revenues lead to growing profits. A business that is growing revenues but unable to grow profits may be a sign that the business is struggling to compete on price or is unable to control its costs.

Sometimes there are valid reasons why a business may grow revenues without growing profits. The business may be investing for the future. Amazon has grown revenues fantastically for years but only in recent years has it become profitable. Nevertheless, investors in Amazon have been richly rewarded because the market recognized that it was more important for Amazon to build out a worldwide infrastructure than it was for the company to chase short-term profit. The infrastructure will support profits long into the future.

Another reason that a business may grow revenues without profits is to drive out competition. A strong business can sell product below cost, forcing weaker competitors into bankruptcy. When the competitors have disappeared, the business can subsequently raise prices and reap the benefits of an enlarged market share.

This tactic can also be used by small companies as a way to gain a foothold in an established market. The business will attract new customers by setting a competitive price. The hope is that the customers will be so impressed by the quality of the product that they will remain customers even though the company later raises prices.

In summary, growing profits are important, but before ruling out a business on that basis, you must decide whether profits have been reduced in the short term for a valid business reason, or whether the lack of profits indicates a genuine weakness in the business.

Strong Cash Flow

"Turnover is vanity, profit is sanity, but cash is reality." —Anon.

Cash is the lifeblood of any business. Some businesses devour cash relentlessly. Airlines and public utilities need to spend large amounts of cash before making a single sale. Other businesses seem to generate cash at will. As an example, a web-based retail business has a low capital requirement, collects cash up front from its customers, and can sit on that cash for up to sixty days before settling with suppliers.

Insurance is another great example of a cash-rich business. The customer pays a premium immediately, but a claim may not occur for months or years, if at all. The excess cash held by insurance companies is known as **float**.

Warren Buffett's massively successful tenure at Berkshire Hathaway has been a result of the outstanding way in which he has invested the float.

To become a successful investor, it is important to understand the difference between cash flow and profit.

Businesses procuring capital assets must lay out large amounts of cash in the short term. For the purpose of calculating profit, accounting rules dictate that the expense must be spread over many years.

This requirement stems from the **accruals principle**, which states that an income or expense should be charged in the period to which it relates, rather than the period in which payment is made. A firm may spend $10M on a factory, which is expected to generate $2M every year for the next ten years. In this case, the period to which the expense relates is the expected lifetime of the factory—ten years.

If the accounts were prepared on a cash basis, the expenses in the first year would be $10M set against the income of $2M, resulting in a loss of $8M. For the remaining nine years, the accounts would show a profit of $2M—as the cost of the factory had been entirely absorbed in the first year.

Preparing the accounts using the accruals principle, the $10M cost of the factory would be spread evenly over the ten years, resulting in an expense of $1M in each year. This would be offset against the income for each year of $2M, resulting in a profit of $1M for each year.

Most accountants would argue that by eradicating the wild swings in years where there is high capital expenditure, we get a better indication of the underlying performance of the business.

If a business receives cash in advance, the rule applies in reverse. For example, a business may sell a maintenance contract, collecting cash up front. The accruals principle dictates that the income must be broken down into separate amounts spread over the lifetime of the contract.

As a result of the application of the accruals principle, the profit shown on a company's books can be widely divergent from the flow of cash received or disbursed. Sometimes it can result in the accounting records presenting a distorted picture of reality. For example, a pipeline company may lay a pipe costing $60M that generates income over the next thirty years. A prudent accountant may decide to depreciate the pipeline over ten years—resulting in a charge to the accounts of $6M per year. If the cost of the pipeline had been spread over the full thirty years, the charge would have been $2M per year—a $4M difference over the first ten years.

This could result in the pipeline company reporting a $2M loss in its accounts, whereas a more realistic calculation would have shown a $2M profit—potentially creating a huge discrepancy in the share price and an opportunity for the knowledgeable!

The apparent discrepancy between cash flow and profit has been used to great effect by John Malone. He used the steady, reliable cash flows from the cable TV business to ratchet up debt and make acquisitions. Malone realized that by concentrating on cash flow, he kickstarted a series of virtuous circles.

By depreciating his assets aggressively, he not only wiped out his reported profit but also his tax liability. This gave him more borrowing power and further scope for acquisitions. By borrowing more, he increased his interest expense, which again he could use to offset more taxes. Because he was expanding rapidly, he had more bargaining power with content providers and was able to buy programs more cheaply, thus releasing further cash for more acquisitions...

Malone's relentless focus on cash at the expense of profit was not viewed favorably by Wall Street, where earnings per share was the preferred metric. But early investors in Malone's business made average annual returns of thirty percent from 1973 until 1998, far outstripping the fourteen percent returned by the S&P 500 over the same period.

Good Return on Capital

Any investment decision must be based on the premise that your funds could not be better used elsewhere.

If you were able to invest cash at zero risk for a return of 2%, why would you make a risky investment in a company that is also likely to return 2%?

Every business has a similar choice. Why would a business make a risky investment in a major factory if it could make a similar return by depositing the money in a bank? Or for that matter, if a business has nothing better to do with its cash than put it in a bank, should it not return that cash as a dividend to its shareholders and let them decide what they want to do with their money?

We give risk capital to businesses in the hope of achieving superior returns. A shareholder, taking on the most risk, will be looking for a return of maybe 10%, 12%, or more.

The capital of a business comes from the issuance of shares and from taking on debt. Over time, the amount of capital available to the business will increase as prior-year profits accumulate and become available for investment.

By taking the profit made by a business and dividing by the amount of capital, we can determine the level of return that the business is achieving from that capital. This figure is known as the **return on capital employed (ROCE)**.

The ROCE is the most basic measure of whether the business is using its resources efficiently.

If a business is not able to deliver an acceptable level of return, taking into account the risk inherent in the business, then its capital—and yours—would be better deployed elsewhere.

Strong Corporate Culture

As investors, we may be tempted to deploy our capital in businesses that prioritize profitability and total shareholder returns.

But the evidence shows that businesses that pay attention to all of their stakeholders, including customers, employees, and suppliers, are more likely to produce better shareholder returns in the long term.

In their seminal 1982 work, 'In Search of Excellence', Tom Peters and Bob Waterman looked at the characteristics of successful American businesses.

They selected thirty-two businesses that met their criteria as "excellent companies." In order to make the selection, they used a number of criteria, including compound asset growth and total return on capital. Peters and Waterman found that the most successful companies had a strong corporate culture. Their internal values were much more likely to be focused on customers, staff, or product quality than they were on profit or shareholders.

Paradoxically, the companies that appeared to care least for their investors ended up producing far better returns for their shareholders than their competitors.

If you had invested $10,000 in the 32 public companies that Peters and Waterman selected, over the following twenty years it would have returned $140,050, as compared to the average market return of $85,500.

The cultural values propounded by Peters and Waterman have strong echoes today in some of the ideas expressed by businessmen like Satya Nadella's transformation of Microsoft's culture around empathy and collaboration, Costco's continued commitment under Ron Vachris to the staff-centered approach and supplier partnerships established by founder Jim Sinegal, or Brian Chesky's obsessive customer focus and attention to culture at Airbnb.

One of the excellent companies selected by Peters and Waterman was IBM—a flagship company for American industry in 1982. Eleven years later, IBM was in trouble. Deep trouble.

IBM needed somebody to turn the business around, and the recipient of the poisoned chalice was one Louis Gerstner.

Gerstner came from a consultancy background with McKinsey—an old-fashioned firm that emphasized hard numbers. When he came to IBM, nobody expected a dramatic turnaround. The market expected the hard-headed Gerstner to analyze the business, pick it apart, and break it up.

Instead, he executed a remarkable turnaround, learning a lot about business and himself in the process. He said:

"Until I came to IBM, I probably would have told you that culture was just one among several important elements in any organization's makeup and success—along with vision, strategy, marketing, financials, and the like... I came to see, in my time at IBM, that culture isn't just one aspect of the game; it is the game. In the end, an organization is nothing more than the collective capacity of its people to create value."

It is true that not all successful companies subscribe to all of these values. Ryanair has had a reputation for treating its customers like cattle. Amazon has been accused of riding roughshod over its staff in its obsession to look after the customer.

But overall, the evidence shows that companies with strong cultural values are more likely to deliver strong, long-term returns to the investor.

Total Addressable Market

In order to achieve superior investment returns, it is necessary for the companies that we invest in to achieve strong growth.

If a company's customers already comprise 90% of the market, it is going to be difficult for that company to grow unless it finds new products to sell or is able to offer its customers compelling upgrades to existing products.

A company with 0.1% of the market that delivers better products than its competitors has the potential to deliver amazing growth.

The total, worldwide value of customer spending for a product or group of products is referred to as the **total addressable market** (**TAM**).

Knowing the TAM allows you to make an assessment about a company's potential for growth. Consider a company that turns over $1M with a total addressable market of $100M. If it is realistic for the company to command a 10% market share, then 10% of the TAM is $10m, and the company could grow to 10 times its current size.

Much of the debate about whether Apple is a good investment centers around analysts' assessments of its room for growth in a market where it already has a dominant position.

Reinvestment Potential

In the last section, we saw how a company's growth potential is affected by the total addressable market for its products.

Another factor that can hamper or aid growth is the ease with which a business can reinvest its earnings.

A fine dining restaurant may get rave reviews because of the unique talents of its chef patron. The TAM for this business may be huge, but it is impossible to grow the business as the chef cannot be replicated. The business may generate lots of cash—but it doesn't have a way to spend it.

On the other hand, a restaurant business selling burgers or burritos has fantastic growth possibilities. Once the management finds a "formula" that resonates with the public, the business can keep adding new restaurants as fast as it can earn the money to pay for them. This is one of the reasons why successful restaurant chains have produced fantastic returns for investors.

Companies may make decent profits, but if they are to grow, there must be a straightforward way for them to reinvest those profits back into the business.

A business which has small revenues in comparison to a large total addressable market, and an easy route to reinvest profits, can deliver huge growth.

Low Capital Requirement

Some businesses require large expenditures of capital in order to generate revenue. Heavy engineering firms, builders, and aircraft companies cannot generate income without first making major investments.

Other companies, such as consultancies or recruitment organizations, require little or no initial capital. These businesses are often referred to as "capital light" industries.

Some organizations position themselves to be capital light. The company responsible for the computer chips that power most smartphones, ARM Holdings, doesn't actually make any chips at all. The chips are designed in-house, and the design is then licensed for manufacture elsewhere.

ARM uses its resources where they can add most value—at the computer workstation designing chips. Offloading the capital risk of manufacture is a smart move. Many other chip designers follow this model—known as fabless manufacturing.

Some companies require a high initial capital investment but have low ongoing capital needs. Firms such as Facebook or LinkedIn initially spend heavily, building a web infrastructure to support millions of users. But once that investment is in place, additional users can be supported at virtually no additional cost.

Software companies spend years developing products, but once a product is complete, it can be sold at a high price with no further expense. (Although modern AI which can write software is potentially disruptive to these companies as applications that took years to write may now be completed in weeks or even days.)

It is easier for a company with a low capital requirement to become profitable than it is for a company with a high capital requirement. Airline companies, with their high capital needs, have had a notorious reputation as unsatisfactory investments. Warren Buffett famously once said of the Wright brothers, "Indeed, if a farsighted capitalist had been present at Kitty Hawk, he would have done his successors a huge favor by shooting Orville down."

A business which has already incurred the lion's share of its required capital expenditure and is now reaping the reward of growing revenues with low ongoing costs can make a particularly attractive investment. For example, a business that has produced a well-received software product has overcome the development risk and can look forward to making high-value sales with fat margins. But the gravy does not last forever—products like this will at some point need to be upgraded and/or eventually replaced, so it is important to establish whether the business is carrying out research and developing for the future.

Personal Experience

An excellent way to evaluate whether a company is a good business is through your own personal experience. This was one of Peter Lynch's favorite strategies. In 'One Up on Wall Street', Lynch writes, "The best place to begin looking for the tenbagger is close to home—if not in the backyard, then down at the shopping mall, and especially wherever you happen to work."

Often, it will be the good personal experience that first alerts you to a business. If you see a long line forming at a restaurant; or if you see a product selling like hotcakes at the local store: this could be your edge over the closeted Wall Street professional.

As soon as you see an opportunity like this, get on the internet and start digging. If the business makes the grade on all the other important metrics, you could be one of the early birds that gets in on the stock before it takes off.

Low Profile

Wall Street analysts tend to concentrate on widely held stocks with a large market capitalization. Some companies can have undervalued stock prices for no other reason than lack of attention. As these companies grow, the street begins to take notice, and their stock prices rise.

When you research a company on the internet, you will usually see an option for "Analyst Coverage." If a business has few analysts listed, that is a good indication of an under-covered stock. For further confirmation, listen to a replay of the latest conference call and note which analysts participate in the questions at the end of the call.

According to the old adage, "Where there's muck, there's brass." One of the peculiarities of the stock market is that many people are put off investing in companies in unattractive industries such as waste disposal, graveyards, or funeral services. (Although they do not quite fit into the "low-profile" category, the much-despised tobacco industry has provided some of the best returns in the stock market.)

Unattractive, under-covered industries may lack the allure of high-tech businesses, but these Cinderella stocks often turn out to be hidden gems. Keep an open mind, and you will be rewarded if you are willing to venture where the squeamish fear to tread.

Special Circumstances

Most businesses come upon hard times at some stage. Sometimes there can be a genuine business problem. Other times there may be an unjustified drop in the stock price.

In 1963, American Express became embroiled in a huge scandal involving non-existent stocks of salad oil held as collateral by one of their borrowers. Consequently, the stock tanked (no pun intended).

While others fled the stock, Warren Buffett looked at the circumstances and decided that this was essentially a good business having bad luck and plowed 40% of his partnership's investments into American Express.

Within a year, the share price had recovered 40% of its value and went on to rise for many years thereafter.

"Short sellers" are market participants that place their trades in reverse. They sell a stock that they do not own, hoping to buy it back later at a lower price (more on this later). Some short sellers perform a useful function—their analysis and research may alert investors to problems which may not have materialized otherwise. But it is unusual for short sellers to be motivated by the desire to be public guardians.

Because share prices are prone to sharp downward movements on bad news, it is easy for a short seller to move a stock price by making vague insinuations. If that stock has enjoyed recent gains, nervous holders (and algo traders) are likely to sell and take profits at the slightest sign of trouble.

Businesses that have enjoyed rapid growth and seen a corresponding increase in their share price are a prime target for short sellers. They will brief friendly journalists to create rumors in the media and write articles on websites such as "Seeking Alpha," often using false names.

Technically speaking, this practice is market manipulation — a prohibited practice that carries heavy penalties. But on a practical level, it is difficult to prove, and very few culprits are prosecuted. This lack of regulatory enforcement allows the short sellers to make easy profits.

Most private, individual investors do not have these methods at their disposal. But the activities of the unscrupulous short seller can create good opportunities for the savvy investor. When a stock that you are following falls through an obvious short attack, spend some time researching the background.

It will often transpire that the bear case is a mishmash of half-truths, non-specific allegations, and maybes.

There is no rush to invest in a company suffering a short attack. Shorts will have a coordinated series of moves over a period of weeks or months. Stock prices go down quickly and may suffer several sharp declines as the shorts release their ammunition.

Once a stock has been tarnished, the market is normally slow to recognize its mistake, and it may take months or even years to recover to a fair valuation. Choose your entry point wisely and allow patience to be rewarded.

Reasonable Share Price

Many novice investors begin their search by looking for "cheap" shares. The great investors—those that we have chosen as the model to use for this book—take the opposite approach. Warren Buffett summed it up nicely: "It's far better to buy a wonderful company at a fair price than a fair company at a wonderful price."

If you should happen to overpay 10% or even 30% today for a business that will compound growth at 20% for the next 20 years, it's hardly a disaster. Would you really prefer to miss out on all those years of stellar growth for the sake of a short-term "saving"?

You may often find that a high-quality business will trade at, say, 25 times earnings while its competitors trade at 16 times earnings. A price-conscious buyer may resolve not to overpay and wait patiently for a chance to buy at 18 times earnings during "a dip."

You may be lucky, and that dip may come next week. Or it may come in two years' time, by which time the shares are now double in value. Or it may never come at all.

That's not to say you should pay "any price" even for a really good business.

A good business that is richly valued presents a difficult buying decision. Is it worth overpaying today for a great business? How will you feel if there is a dip in the market next week and the price falls by half? But on the other hand, what if no dip comes and the price sails into the stratosphere before you have another chance to buy?

There is no straight answer, and how you handle questions like these will shape your future as an investor.

If you really like a business, the best approach is to take a small stake and add to it over time at better value points.

We will take a much closer look at how you should value a business later in the book.

Summary

In this chapter, we have looked at the various criteria that we can use to evaluate a business as a potential investment. We started by looking at the single most important attribute that separates the winning businesses from the rest—competitive advantage.

Companies with competitive advantage can be thought of as one of the following:

- Disruptive Innovators
- Sustaining Innovators
- Financial Engineers
- Brilliant Executors
- IP Kings

Following our examination of competitive advantage, we looked at the other important factors that enable us to identify superior businesses:

- Good Management
- Strong Balance Sheet
- Growing Revenues
- Growing Profitability
- Strong Cash Flow
- Good Return on Capital
- Strong Corporate Culture
- Total Addressable Market
- Reinvestment Potential
- Low Capital Requirement
- Personal Experience
- Low Profile
- Special Circumstances

- Reasonable Share Price

It is unlikely that a business will get a 100% pass on all of these points. But each time that you add a mental "tick in the box," the investment case grows. Not all investors would weight these factors in the same way. But most would agree that good management is essential. And most would have their strongest weightings near the top of the list.

This has been a long chapter. But that's because the material here goes to the heart of what investing is all about — understanding business — knowing what makes one business different from another — assessing relative strengths and weaknesses — and ultimately, separating the winners from the losers.

Warren Buffett says, "I am a better investor because I am a businessman, and a better businessman because I am an investor."

Perhaps the most important lesson we can learn as investors is to always strive to think like a businessman.

Does the Story Make Sense?

The Why and the Wherefore

As you should know by now, a stock is not a lottery ticket but a share of a real business.

And every business has a story.

Peter Lynch describes it like this:

"Getting the story on a company is a lot easier if you understand the basic business. That's why I'd rather invest in panty hose than in communications satellites, or in hotel chains than in fiber optics. The simpler it is, the better I like it. When somebody says, 'Any idiot could run this joint,' that's a plus as far as I'm concerned, because sooner or later any idiot probably is going to be running it."

Lynch later equates "the story" to what he calls his "two-minute drill"—a brief explanation as to why this particular stock makes a good investment.

If you cannot put together a brief, simple explanation as to why you should be investing in a company, then you have no real case for investment. Or as Lynch says, "Once you are able to tell the story... so that even a child could understand it, then you have a proper grasp of the situation."

These days, the story is often referred to as the **investment thesis**.

Some stories offer the promise of great reward. But the rules of risk and reward dictate that these investments will also have a significant potential for failure.

Take the case of two companies: Westport Innovations and Tesla Motors. This is what I wrote about these companies back in 2016 in my book 'How to Make a Million':

Westport designs and makes fuel injector systems that allow engines to run on natural gas instead of diesel. In the early part of 2012, crude oil prices were $111 a barrel, and natural gas was trading at less than $2 per Mcf. The practical consequence of this was that the cost of running a truck on natural gas was considerably cheaper than the cost of running on diesel.

The downside was that a truck equipped to use natural gas was significantly more expensive. But as most trucks are used heavily, a truck running on natural gas instead of diesel would achieve a payback in less than 2 years.

With a considerable economic incentive to convert to natural gas, many forecasters were projecting that a large percentage of heavy trucks would convert to natural gas from diesel—resulting in huge growth for Westport. The share price was trading at over $42, with some analysts predicting huge gains.

Truck owners are conservative by nature, and progress in converting to natural gas was slow. The engines Westport supported were not quite the right size. Demand slackened as the market waited for bigger, more efficient engines to become available. Then the price of oil began to fall...

Westport's bright hopes all but evaporated. The company struggled to limit cash burn and contain costs. In early 2016, the share price had fallen from over $42 to less than $2.

The original investment thesis was sound. But subsequent events conspired to turn a potential multi-bagger investment into a financial catastrophe.

At around the same time, Tesla Motors was ramping up production of its new electric car — the Model S.

Earlier electric cars had failed because it was uneconomic to produce a battery large enough to give the car meaningful range. Tesla's strategy was to produce a high-end car, competing with expensive BMWs and Mercedes. Because the car was already expensive, the cost of the battery would be less significant in proportion to the overall vehicle.

Tesla's strategy was extremely risky. How could a company with no experience of designing cars hope to compete with companies like BMW and Mercedes? And on top of that, they would have to convince customers to put up with the inconvenience of a slow-charging battery with limited places to charge. When the price of oil started to fall, many skeptics concluded that Tesla's prospects were bleak.

But the critics were confounded. Demand for the new Model S was huge. Shares in Tesla traded at around $27 at the beginning of 2012. By the middle of 2015, they reached a high of over $280—a tenfold increase in just over three years!

Yet at the outset of 2012, many a thoughtful investor would have given Westport a much greater chance of achieving success than Tesla. The case for Westport was based on simple economics. Tesla needed to convince customers to radically alter their approach to motoring—a much tougher ask.

The lesson here is that however sensible a story might seem, there is no guarantee of the outcome — or at what point another twist might happen. Who knows whether in ten years' time Westport will have grown into a huge business and Tesla may have withered on the vine? Unlikely, but not impossible.

In hindsight, you might conclude that Tesla had one great advantage in their favor—their visionary CEO, Elon Musk—yet another reminder that the importance of leadership cannot be overstated.

Update from 2026: Looking back from today's vantage point, the contrast between these two companies has become even starker. Westport struggled for years and eventually pivoted its business model, never recovering its 2012 highs. Tesla, on the other hand, went on to become one of the most valuable companies in the world. By 2025, Tesla's market capitalization exceeded that of most traditional automakers combined—vindicating the early investors who saw past the short-term skepticism to recognize the transformative potential of Musk's vision. The lesson? Sometimes the "riskier" bet on exceptional leadership and disruptive innovation pays off far better than the "safer" bet on simple economics.

One common thread shared by Tesla and Westport is that neither of them were making money.

The company with the better “story"— Westport — was the company that failed to reach its potential.

Companies that are all "story" with no earnings are fraught with risk. Even the most compelling story can fall apart when unforeseen difficulties arise and funds dwindle.

Warren Buffett is not immune to sometimes making an outside bet on a company with a good story— he invested in a Chinese electric car company, for heaven's sake! But the vast majority of his capital is deployed investing in businesses with solid, growing earnings.

Lynch puts it succinctly: "... it always comes down to earnings and assets. Especially earnings."

In 'One Up on Wall Street', Lynch sets out the story behind one of his favorite investments. La Quinta Hotels was building hotels without wedding areas, conference rooms, reception areas, kitchens, or restaurants. They situated the hotels next to 24-hour restaurants — so that the residents had ready access to food. Sound familiar? There are numerous "express" hotel chains exploiting this concept today, but back in the late '70s it was unheard of.

Lynch saw that by doing this, they could offer rooms of equivalent quality to "The Holiday Inn," charge 30% less, and make a greater return. Furthermore, the company was already showing great earnings and growing like a weed.

This is a fine example of a good story — simple to understand, great earnings, no debt, and limited risk.

In the last chapter, we looked at the various qualities that a company should possess in order to qualify for investment.

But investing is about the future, and attributes of excellence in themselves hold no guarantee of what lies ahead. There were many stagecoach builders, gramophone makers, and floppy disk manufacturers that were all excellent in their day.

We have seen here how all these attributes should be wrapped up in a story. A story that makes sense, is simple to understand, and leads to growing earnings.

Which makes this a good point to take a closer look at earnings and how they relate to all the other numbers to be found in a company's financial statements.

Understanding the Numbers

Introduction

Investing is often perceived as a pastime that involves complicated and detailed numeric calculations. Not many of us enjoy working with numbers — if you are one of those lucky few, congratulations.

The good news for the rest of us is that to be a successful investor, you don't need any special facility with mathematics. If you can add, subtract, divide, and multiply, that is all the mathematical knowledge you will ever need.

There is no getting away from the fact that investing is a numbers-based pastime—share prices, revenues, and cash balances are all intrinsically numeric properties.

But finding meaning in these numbers requires very little numeric dexterity. All that is needed is good, old-fashioned common sense.

There are two parts to an investment thesis: "Does the story make sense?" and "Do the numbers add up?" If either of these questions returns a negative, then the thesis is broken. In this chapter, we will address the latter question.

Do the Numbers Add Up?

In this context, making sure the numbers "add up" is shorthand for saying: Do the company's financial reports present a reasonable picture? And in the light of this: Is the company fairly valued?

We will look at valuation in more detail in the next chapter. For now, let's concentrate on how we can interpret the financial statements produced by a business.

Financial statements can seem quite intimidating to an inexperienced investor. The very idea that accountants have spent years of study in order to become qualified to produce these reports adds an aura of mystique. And the jargon one hears amongst professionals discussing financials can sound esoteric and unintelligible.

But in reality, most financial statements are quite straightforward to understand. Many things that we are unfamiliar with seem a little strange and intimidating at first, but once you gain a little familiarity with the layout and terminology, financial statements are no more difficult to understand than a recipe for fruit cake.

Every publicly quoted company must produce an annual report. The annual report contains general information about the business together with detailed financial statements. Further reporting requirements will be set by the country and stock exchange in which the company lists its shares.

In the USA, the Securities and Exchange Commission (SEC) requires companies to submit interim reports quarterly. In the European Union, companies are required to submit interim reports every half year.

The most important sources of information for the investor are the regulatory reports filed by the business. In the early stage of getting to know a business, the annual report is the best place to start. The business will explain what it does, outline its philosophy, and give detailed financial results for the previous year.

Management will often have its own ideas about those areas where investors should focus their attention. Consequently, annual reports often contain selected financial highlights in the glossy pages at the front, with the detailed financial information hidden away at the end. In a similar fashion, interim reports are often accompanied by a press release with the metrics favored by management set out boldly at the front, with the accompanying detail consigned to the small print at the end.

When you are looking at financial data, it is usually best to ignore the selected highlights and headlines and instead look at the reports that have been prepared as required by regulation. Go to the audited financial statements at the back of the annual report, or seek out the quarterly figures on the 10Q form submitted to the SEC (or equivalent).

A company's financial statements come in three parts:

- Income Statement
- Balance Sheet
- Cash Flow Statement

These three reports address the three key questions:

- Is the business making money?
- Does it have sufficient resources to pay its bills?
- What is it doing with its cash?

We will spend some time looking at each of these three statements.

Let's start with the most important.

The Income Statement

The Income Statement sets out all the income received and expenditure incurred by a business over a set period. (It may also be referred to as the Profit and Loss Statement or Profit and Loss Account).

If the income received by a business is greater than the expenditure incurred, the business is making a profit - the amount of profit being the difference between income and expenditure. If expenditure exceeds income, the difference is negative and the business is making a loss.The general format of the income statement is shown in Figure One.

Company Name
Income Statement

	Period ended December 2025
Revenue	
Main Product Sales	$ 200,000
Other types of Sales	100,000
Total Revenue	300,000
Operating Costs and expenses:	
Cost of sales	100,000
Other Costs	40,000
Total operating costs and expenses	140,000
Income from Operations	160,000
Non-Operational Expenses	
Interest	20,000
Taxes	40,000
Total Non-Operational Expenses	60,000
Net Earnings	$ 100,000

Figure One

Businesses produce an income statement at the end of each financial year[1]. Businesses may also produce an interim income statement showing the results for the previous three months, or six months.

In financial statements, the total sales (or 'takings') is usually described as **Revenue**.

The income statement shows the revenue at the top, which may be subdivided into different categories of revenue.

[1] Companies do not always end their reporting year at the end of December - they may choose any month. The term financial year is used simply to differentiate between a company's reporting year and the calendar year. A financial year is still a year in length. Occasionally, companies may report over a shorter or longer period to accommodate a change to their reporting month.

Beneath the revenue, the income statement lists the costs that the business has incurred.

The costs are deducted from the revenue in order to calculate the profit that the business has achieved.

Often the business may break down the costs into various categories. Costs related to the normal operation of the business may be listed first and deducted from revenue to produce a figure for the operating profit, or **Operating Income**.

Finally, any costs that are not related to normal operations are deducted to result in a final profit figure, usually described as **Net Income**.

At first glance, financial statements can be intimidating for the novice investor. But as with most unfamiliar things within a very short period of time you will get used to the format and the jargon and wonder what all the fuss was about. Interpreting them successfully is largely a matter of gaining familiarity and using simple common sense. For any particular business under consideration, there will usually be a few obvious questions that arise. Such as:

- Is the company growing?
- How does the business spend its money?
- How does it compare with its competitors?

The Income Statement addresses the important question, 'Is the business making money?'.

The next question we might ask is, 'Does the business have sufficient resources to pay its bills?'.

To answer this question, we need to examine the Balance Sheet.

The Balance Sheet

Overview

The very name 'Balance Sheet' straight away suggests some questions to the enquiring mind. Why 'balance sheet'? What is it that balances? And why the need to balance in the first place?

Let's take a little time to review some of the very basics of accounting. Not everybody's idea of excitement, but just a little time spent getting a firm grasp of some very basic concepts makes life much easier when trying to understand financial statements. And understanding financial statements is a fundamental necessity for the successful investor.

The concept of a balance sheet takes us back to the origin of modern bookkeeping, as described by the Franciscan friar, Luca Pacioli in 1494. His method for accounting for commercial transactions was simple, inspired, and elegant.

Each transaction has two sides. If you pay money into your business the business acquires an **asset** - the cash. But at the same time the business also acquires a **liability** - it owes you the money. **Assets** and **Liabilities** are two of the primary types of accounting entries.

Another type of transaction, occurs when you sell something, for example if you sell a product for $100 you register an **income** $100 and at the same time you gain an **asset**, perhaps cash of $100, or is you sell on credit a customer has a debt of $100.

Or you might incur an **expense** such as a rental bill. The two sides of this transaction are the **expense** on one hand and the **liability** to the landlord on the other.

There are four types of accounting entry, and every transaction can be recorded using these four types - Assets, Liabilities, Income and Expenses.

Assets and **Expenses** are recorded as **Debits. Liabilities** and **Income** are recorded as **Credits**.

The Income and Expenses are shown on the Income Statement (which we have just covered).

The Assets and Liabilities are shown on the balance sheet.

The Balance Sheet asset accounts represent things that are owned such as cash, buildings, inventory, debts due from customers. The liability accounts represent things that are owed - long-term loans, rent outstanding, amounts owed to suppliers.

Because every transaction is entered as a debit and a credit, all the debits and the credits in the accounts will always balance to zero. This is a wondrous thing. It provides a basic controlling framework that makes it difficult for an unscrupulous person to artificially inflate sales or mis-state profits. Any suspect entry made in one of the income or expense accounts will automatically throw up an unexpected entry in the balance sheet. And that should give rise to a query[2].

In the days of manual ledgers, accounts that did not balance were often the first indication that an error had been made and bookkeepers and accountants would routinely spend many days every month meticulously reconciling their accounts to balance their month-end ledgers.

At the end of the year all of the income and expenses will have been entered into the ledger as debit and credit entries. The difference between the total income of a business and its total expenditure is its profit. If the sum of all these entries is a credit balance, then the business has made a profit - if it is a debit balance then it has made a loss.

---

[2] Double entry bookkeeping makes it more difficult to misrepresent the financials, but it is not a perfect protection against a determined fraudster - as a long history of infamous cases shows.

Once a business has produced its end of year accounts, the entries on the income and expenses accounts need to be cleared so as to start the next year afresh - but we cannot simply delete them as it would break the rules of bookkeeping.

The profit generated by the business is the amount owed to the owners of the business for their investment. This is recognized by transferring all of the balances from the individual income and expense accounts to the equity account. At this point there are no remaining balances in the income and expense accounts, and the sum total of all the asset and liability accounts amounts to zero - as it must.

The Balance Sheet is simply a listing of the accounts, formatted so as to show the asset and liability accounts separately. At the time when the Balance Sheet is produced, there are no balances on the income and expenditure accounts as they have already been transferred to the equity account. The assets are the debit balances. The liabilities are the credit balances. The total of the assets must equal the total of the liabilities as overall the debit balances and credit balances cancel out to zero. Thus the balance sheet balances, and that is why it is called a balance sheet.

As each year progresses, if a company is profitable, we would expect its assets to increase. The increase in the asset accounts (debit balances) must equal the increase in credits transferred in to the equity account from the profit and loss accounts.[3]

The structure of most balance sheets is something along the lines of the example shown in Figure Two.

---

[3] For a small business with poor accounting, it is possible to calculate the profit for the year with no formal profit and loss accounting at all, simply by looking at the increase in the assets (balance sheet debits). That is how accountants prepare figures for disorganized small businesses with little formal records.

Company Name **Balance Sheet**	**As at** **December 2025**	
Assets		
Current Assets:		
Cash	300	(3)
Short Term Investments	100	(4)
Accounts Receivable	600	(5)
Inventory	300	(6)
Total Current Assets	1,300	(7)
Long Term Assets:		
Fixed Assets		
Property	1,000	(11)
Plant and Machinery	300	(12)
Intangible Assets		
Goodwill	200	(14)
Intellectual Property	100	(13)
Total Long Term Assets	1,700	
TOTAL ASSETS	**$ 3,000**	
Liabilities and Equity		
Current Liabilities:		
Accounts Payable	400	(9)
Other Amounts Due Within One Year	100	(10)
Total Current Liabilities	500	(8)
Long Term Liabilities:		
Long term Debt	200	(15)
Total Liabilities	700	
Shareholder Equity:		
Initial Shareholder Capital	400	(1)
Retained Earnings	1,900	(2)
Total Shareholder Equity	2,300	
TOTAL LIABILITIES AND EQUITY	**$ 3000**	

Figure Two

We will go through the various asset categories in turn.

First, let's turn our attention to the section headed Shareholder Equity. It has been broken down into two separate totals for 'Initial Shareholder Capital' and 'Retained Earnings' (marked (1) and (2) on the right of Figure Two).

Companies like to report the amount contributed as initial capital separately from the accumulated profits, so instead of having one **Equity** account, we have two accounts: **Initial Capital** and **Retained Earnings**. (Some businesses also split retained earnings again to show the current year profit).

The important point to grasp is this: The total amount owed by a business to its shareholders is equal to the capital contributed by the shareholders (shares issued) plus all the accumulated profits made to date.

That is one way we can define what the business owes the shareholders. But because the total accumulated capital and profit is always balanced by all the balance sheet figures, we can also look at it from another angle.

The amount the business owes to its shareholders - *the shareholders' equity in the business* - is equivalent to the sum of all the cash balances, debtors, stock, property, and other assets of the business less any amounts the business owes to banks, trade creditors, and other liabilities - *the net assets of the business.*

Shareholders Equity = Net Assets

(You may have noticed that this is not the way in which the information is presented on our example Balance Sheet which follows the general reporting convention in the U.S.A. This is not always the case as we will discuss later.)

An examination of the constituent parts of a balance sheet can give us a much better understanding of how a business is performing. To really understand what a balance sheet is telling us, we have to put ourselves in the place of the management of the business.

If you already run a business, you will understand the day to day issues of managing cash flow. If not, take a moment to imagine what it is like. Your customers may be strapped for cash and evasive when you chase them for payment. Your suppliers may demand that their bills be paid - and you can't afford to be without supplies. The tax man will require payment at the due date or you will face punitive fines or worse. Your staff must be paid on time, month in month out.

For the business to run smoothly, it is important to have enough cash to meet your day to day liabilities comfortably. What if an unforeseen event occurs? You may suddenly find that your incoming cash dries up, but your suppliers, the tax man, and, most importantly, your staff must all be paid on time.

If a business is growing - opening new locations, taking on new staff, commissioning equipment - then a further strain will be placed on the cash position.

These are the sort of issues that you should have in mind when you look at a balance sheet. Put yourself in the place of the business. Does the business have lots of cash? How much does the business owe suppliers?

When we look at the cash position it is not only the cash in the bank that matters We also need to consider things that will become cash in the near future (marked (3) and (4) on the example). Tradable investments, short term deposits or any asset that can be turned into cash can be thought of as equivalent to cash. Trade debtors (shown as Accounts Receivable (5)) are likely to settle their bills in the coming weeks or months, so we can think of debtors as nearly as good as cash (there is still some uncertainty as to whether they are all able to pay on time - or at all).

Inventory (see (6)) can be sold in the near future, and we can reasonably expect that it will become cash in the near term. But there is more uncertainty about inventory than accounts receivable. In the first place the inventory in question might be unsaleable for some reason (it may be unfashionable, or defective, or it may be in a store with an ineffective sales person). In the second place if inventory is sold on credit, the asset will then effectively become a debtor - and we are still left with the uncertainty of collecting payment.

If a company holds inventory that cannot be sold easily it should not be shown on the balance sheet - but a company struggling for liquidity cannot always be relied upon to be fastidious in identifying obsolescent inventory so it is always wise to be sceptical in assessing an inventory figure.

Assets that are cash or likely to become cash soon are classified as **Current Assets** (shown in total (7)).

Current assets are important because they can be used to settle those liabilities that are due in the near future - correspondingly referred to as **Current Liabilities** (see (8)).

Current liabilities will include trade creditors (shown as Accounts Payable (9)), bank overdrafts, short term loans, or any payment due in the near term such as a fine or tax bill (see (10)).

When considering a company for investment, one of the first things that many investors look at is the cash figure on the balance sheet.

(In 'One up on Wall Street', Peter Lynch states that he first looks at the cash, and then long-term debt - and he pretty much ignores everything else.)

Consider a business that immediately grinds to a halt - no further sales and no further expenses. The remaining inventory is sold and the outstanding trade debts are collected. Is there enough to pay off the creditors? In other words, do the current assets exceed the current liabilities?

The ratio of current assets divided by current liabilities is called the **Current Ratio** - it is commonly used in financial circles to assess whether a company has a stable cash position - otherwise referred to as a company's **Liquidity**. (For the example Balance Sheet, the Current Ratio would be 1,300 / 500 = 2.6)

Because of the problems associated with inventory, many investors also look at a stricter test - the ratio of Cash plus Trade Debtors over Current Liabilities - known as the **Quick Ratio** or **Acid Test**. (For our example Balance Sheet the

Quick Ratio would be (300 + 100 + 600) / 500 = 2 - note that we have treated Short Term Investments as Cash.)

If a company that has a good current ratio (significantly more than one) or even better, a good quick ratio, that is usually considered to be a positive sign. But it is not imperative for a company to have current assets in excess of current liabilities.

Imagine a business with a cash balance that is always zero. Every day the money collected from debtors or through cash sales is just enough to pay the bills.

It doesn't matter whether the value of current assets exceeds current liabilities. As long as the business remains in balance the bills are paid out of ongoing cashflow and everything is fine.

But problems arise if things don't go as expected. Because things are so finely balanced, it just takes one bad day and the business is not able to meet its liabilities.

Cash is important because it tells you how well the company is positioned to withstand unexpected events.

If there is any problem with collecting cash, the balance in the bank account can be used to 'take up the slack' and keep making payments until the problem has been resolved.

The interplay between cash, debtors, creditors and inventory can be thought of as the circulation driven by the beating heart of the business. It represents the capital employed every day in order to make the business work and it is referred to as **Working Capital**. A healthy business requires good management of working capital. (For our example Balance Sheet the total working capital employed is the total of current assets less current liabilities = 1,300 - 500 = $800.)

When you look at a balance sheet, the relative amounts of cash, debtors, creditors and inventory are not so important. Every business will have a different balance. But any *changes* in the relationship between the various working capital accounts can be a sign that something different is happening to the business. If a business traditionally has high amounts of cash and low trade creditors, and you notice that suddenly cash balances are deteriorating and creditors are increasing, that is a major warning that things are going badly.

It is easier for a business to disguise poor performance in the income statement than it is in the balance sheet. By adjusting a few provisions or recognising income early a company may get away with a little window dressing in the income statement - at least in the short term. But problems on the balance sheet are harder to disguise.

Detecting a problem in working capital may be as straightforward as finding a deteriorating cash balance - or you may see it as an unusual increase in creditors (the company is stringing out its suppliers) or a reduction in debtors (the company may be arm-twisting its customers).

In ordinary circumstances keeping your debtors at a low level and gaining maximum benefit from credit are good things - showing shrewd husbandry. It is all a matter of context and interpretation. Suffice it to say that when unusual changes in working capital occur it is a good idea to find out why.

Let's turn our attention now to the other items on the balance sheet - Long-term Assets and Liabilities.

Long-term Assets

Long-term assets fall into two groups. Property and capital equipment such as buildings, plant and machinery - often called **Fixed Assets** (see (11) and (12)), and non-physical assets, otherwise known as **Intangible Assets**.

Let's consider the accounting treatment for fixed assets.

If a business with sales of, say, $1,000,000 and a net profit of $100,000 buys a building for $500,000, then you might think that the additional expenditure would immediately turn that profit of $100,000 into a loss of $400,000. ($100,000 profit - $500,000).

This would give a very misleading picture of the business because the building will be of value to the business not just for this year, but for many years to come. So instead of showing a large expense in the year of purchase, the cost of the building is added as an asset to the balance sheet.

If the building is expected to last for 50 years, it will decrease in value by $10,000 per year ($500,000 divided by 50). In the first year the accounts will show a charge against profit of $10,000, and the asset value on the balance sheet will be shown as $490,000 - being $500,000 for the initial purchase less $10,000 for the loss in value. The loss in value of an asset during a financial reporting period is referred to as **Depreciation**.

In each following year for the next 50 years the value of the asset on the balance sheet will reduce by $10,000. Correspondingly, there will be an expense of $10,000 deducted from the profit in each year. (If you remember from our discussion on bookkeeping a credit to an asset account reduces its balance and a debit to an expense account increases the expense - so the accounting is beautifully straightforward).

Buildings depreciate over long periods - but other assets will be depreciated over shorter periods. The rate of depreciation should match the expected useful life of the asset. A company may determine that its computers will be obsolete after 3 years - so in that case it would be appropriate to depreciate computers at $33^1/_3$% per year. Another business might assess that its industrial plant has an expected life of ten years - so in that case it would be appropriate to depreciate the plant at 10% per year.

Often, a business will acquire a building and depreciate it in the accounts over time, while in reality the value of that building is increasing, rather than decreasing. This can be very useful to an investor, as a business can have underlying assets far more valuable than its accounts suggest.

Value investors use this approach extensively to find investment opportunities. They look for assets that are undervalued on the company's books. This not only applies to property, but to any asset accounted for 'at cost'. Warren Buffett studied this type of investing under the pupillage of Benjamin Graham in his early years and built his reputation by investing in businesses with undervalued assets.

A hefty fixed asset balance represents a backstop for a failing business. If a business is in trouble, in the last resort it can wind down trading and sell off its assets. If the assets are undervalued in the books of account the shareholders will receive a 'surprise' bonus from the sale of assets when the business ceases operation.

Buffett may have been a value investor in his early years, but changed considerably as he learned more about investing and his style matured. The successful investors that we have used as the template for this book look for quality businesses rather than for hidden asset value.

Looking for undervalued assets may not be regarded as a preferred, primary strategy in current times. For one thing, the information that Buffett would dig out painstakingly is now readily available to all and sundry at the touch of a button. But nevertheless, an undervalued asset portfolio may provide strong support to a primary investment thesis.

For example, 'Dollar General' has been a compelling growth story for investors, expanding from around 12,000 stores in the mid-2010s to over 20,000 locations today by serving underserved rural and lower-income communities. Yet beneath this growth narrative lies a substantial owned real estate portfolio that provides a floor for the stock's valuation should the company's expansion eventually plateau.

Fixed assets represent 'locked-up' capital. By this we mean capital that cannot be used more efficiently in other areas of the business. For example, compare the returns received from investing $100,000 in property as against the returns received from using the money to purchase inventory for resale. If the inventory is sold at a 100% markup over the next three months, then the money invested in inventory is making an equivalent annual return of 400%. The money invested in property may be providing some support for the business. And perhaps, over time, the property may appreciate modestly. But the returns achieved will still pale into insignificance compared to the returns achieved by ploughing the money into working capital.

The clue is in the name: *working* capital.

Consider a business that owns a chain of hotels. It has thousands of properties, all acquired at huge cost. It would like to expand, but finds that raising finance is difficult or expensive. How about selling all its hotels to a property company, leasing them back, and using the cash generated to double its hotel count and double its profits?

These are the sorts of questions that should be prompted by a balance sheet with high property values. A fat property portfolio may give some comfort to the value investor. But for an investor looking for high-quality, growing businesses it can be a sign that the business is not making the best use of the capital available.

A business that discloses high values for plant and equipment in its fixed assets raises different questions. Plant and equipment may be a fixed asset but it is more akin to working capital - it is actively used to generate revenue. But plant requires more attention than property. What is the replacement schedule? What provisions have been made for on-going maintenance?

Airlines provide a classic example of an industry that must deal with the issues associated with high equipment cost. Richard Branson said, 'If you want to be a Millionaire, start with a billion dollars and launch a new airline'. It is not impossible for businesses with high asset costs to be profitable, but they do present a whole range of issues that investors must consider.

Another issue with businesses having high equipment costs is that they often need to finance their assets with debt. They may be vulnerable to creditors should revenue falter or interest rates rise.

In contrast to fixed assets, which have an obvious physical purpose and can be seen to contribute to revenue, intangible assets are entirely abstract.

It is tempting to regard intangible assets as a wishy-washy concept invented by accountants. But they can have real value. Intangible assets fall into two general categories: patents and copyright - generally referred to as intellectual property (IP) (see (13) on the example); and goodwill (see (14) on the example).

Ownership of IP gives the business exclusive right to manufacture a product or to use a particular process. If the product is a whole unique product - such as the process for making the sole drug available to cure a particular disease, then the business can set its own price - a massive advantage. More usually the IP will give the business a better way of making a particular component. Competitors will then have to find their own ways of achieving the same result. Copyright in a software product prevents competitors from using the same source code, but does not prevent them from producing a product with equivalent functionality.

IP is an important part of a company's **moat**. The term moat is used to express how difficult it would be for another business to set up as a competitor. Moat gives a company pricing power, which in turn leads to higher margins and in consequence, higher profitability.

Goodwill arises when one business purchases another. The amount of Goodwill is the excess amount paid over the value of the acquired company's assets.

The easiest way to understand goodwill is by way of an example.

Imagine that you know the owner of a hot dog stand in a popular location. The stand is very busy, selling 500 hot dogs a day at $2 each. The wages for the attendant are $200 a day with the cost of ingredients estimated at $200. With total sales of $1,000 (500 X $2) and costs of $400 ($200 wages + $200 ingredients), the estimated daily profit is $600.

Deciding that you are interested in purchasing this attractive looking business, you approach the owner and ask to see his accounts. As he draws out all the cash as income, the only item on his balance sheet is a hot dog stand that has been depreciated with an outstanding balance of $150.

So you have a business with a book value of $150 that produces $600 per day in profit. What would you pay for the business? Whatever amount you suggest, it is likely to be some distance north of $150. Let's assume that you get it at a steal for $5,000.

When you incorporate that business into your own accounts, you can add the hot dog stand as an asset of $150 on your balance sheet. But how do you account for the other $4,850? It will appear as Goodwill.

Does this asset have value? As it produces $600 *per day* it has great value. It is easy to be sceptical about the value of intangible assets in general, and goodwill in particular, but often a factory full of plant designed to produce a product that no longer sells is of far less economic value than an amount paid for goodwill to purchase a great commercial brand.

When Warren Buffett was considering the purchase of See's Candies he was reticent to pay $25 million for a business with $8million of tangible assets, but with encouragement from Charlie Munger, he came around to the idea, marking a change in his investment style and the foundation for his later success. Writing later Buffett wrote, 'Thus our first lesson: businesses logically are worth far more than net tangible assets when they can be expected to produce earnings on such assets considerably in excess of market rates of return. The capitalized value of this excess return is economic Goodwill'.

The amount paid for goodwill is generally reduced over time by way of a charge to profit. This reduction in goodwill is called **Amortization** (being equivalent to depreciation for tangible assets).

It has been known - frequently - for acquisitions to go wrong. What would happen if our newly acquired hot dog business was suddenly served with a notice from the local authority preventing it from selling hot dogs in a public place? Our $4,850 of economic goodwill is suddenly worthless. We would have to write this balance down to zero - a sudden devaluation of goodwill is called an **impairment charge**.

Impairment charges are a lot more common than we would hope, particularly in the accounts of companies with a penchant for acquisition.

Long-term Liabilities

Long-term liabilities comprise any amounts that are due to be paid more than a year from the current reporting date.

Some expenses such as rent or tax, involve agreements that extend over a long period. It may be prudent to recognize these expenses as a charge against current profit notwithstanding that payment will not be made within the next year. These will be shown as deferred expenses under Long-term Liabilities

The more important items that appear under long-term liabilities are long-term loans (see (15) on the example Balance Sheet).

Debt is a bad thing. We know that don't we? Or do we? Often debt can make a serious positive difference to the returns enjoyed by an investor. Let's take an example.

A company wishes to invest in a new venture with a capital cost of $1,000,000 and is expected to make a return of 12% per annum. It finances the venture by issuing 100,000 shares priced at $10 per share. The venture performs successfully and the shareholders are happy with their 12% return of $1.20 per share.

But what if the company had used debt instead? If the company had issued loan stock at a rate of 6% for 80% of the capital and 20,000 shares at $10 what would be the result? Out of the total profit of $120,000 it would require $48,000 to pay the interest. (80% of $1M is $800,000 and 6% of $800,000 is $48,000.) After deducting the $48,000 interest from the $120,000 profit we are left with $72,000 to be distributed among 20,000 shares at $3.60 per share. By using debt the shareholders get *three times the return.*

Of course, that still leaves the problem of repaying the debt. If the venture is ongoing the debt can be rolled forward. If it is not an ongoing venture, the business can sell its assets to recover the capital and pay off the shareholders and the debt holders. (In reality, the situation would be more complex as the resale value of the equipment is not assured. But in principle it is evident that use of debt can juice shareholder returns significantly.)

If debt is so good why don't businesses operate on 1% equity and 99% debt?

Debt is risky. If a business comes across hard times, it can suspend dividend payments to shareholders (if it makes any in the first place). Shareholders have no option but to accept the situation or sell (to a new shareholder, who must also accept the situation). If a business is unable to meet interest payment on a debt, the debt holder can petition for the company to be wound up - or more likely for the company to be restructured so that the shareholders are wiped out and the debt holders gain control.

Debt has a fixed term, so that at some point the debt will either have to be rolled over or repaid. In most cases at least some of the debt will need to be rolled over. If interest rates have risen, or if the company's credit rating has suffered, the new debt could be at substantially higher interest rates than the old debt. This can have a serious effect on the company's profitability.

Wise use of debt can be a valuable way of increasing shareholder returns. Reckless use of debt can be fatal.

Balance Sheet Structure

Let's consider the Balance Sheet structure. If we strip out the detail in our example template, we have the balance sheet shown in Figure Three.

Example Accounts Inc. Balance Sheet	**As at December 2025**
Assets:	
Total Current Assets	1,300
Total Long Term Assets	1,700
TOTAL ASSETS	**$ 3,000**
Liabilities and Equity:	
Total Current Liabilities	500
Long Term Liabilities	200
Total Liabilities	700
Total Shareholder Equity	2,300
TOTAL LIABILITIES AND EQUITY	**$ 3000**

Figure Three

The two totals that balance are 'Total Assets' of $3,000 and 'Total Liabilities and Equity' of $3,000.

We could have chosen to format the balance sheet a different way, as shown in Figure Four.

Example Accounts Inc.

Balance Sheet

	As at December 2025
Assets:	
Total Current Assets	1,300
Total Long Term Assets	1,700
Total Assets	3,000
LESS:	
Total Current Liabilities	500
Long Term Liabilities	200
Total Liabilities	700
NET ASSETS	**$ 2,300**
TOTAL SHAREHOLDER EQUITY	**$ 2,300**

Figure Four

It is conventional in the United States to construct a balance sheet as shown in Figure Three - balancing Total Assets against Equity plus Liabilities. In some jurisdictions, such as in the UK, it is common to show a firm's Net Assets on one side, balanced by the shareholders equity on the other side as shown in Figure Four. Neither approach is more 'correct' than the other. Those who prefer to offset Total Assets against Liabilities plus Equity would defend that presentation by saying that it shows how the assets have been financed.

You may also come across a Balance Sheet format whereby 'Equity plus Long-term Liabilities' are balanced against 'Total Assets Less Current Liabilities' - another approach to the 'financing' side being offset against the 'working' side. Again, this is just a matter of preference and is of no real importance.

The balance sheet is a snapshot. It shows the position of the business at a single point in time. It does not show how well the business generates cash. And it does not give us an answer to the last of the three questions that we posed right at the start of this chapter: 'What is the business doing with its cash?'.

To address that question, lets's move on to the final part of the jigsaw.

The Cash Flow Statement

At first you may wonder why we need a cash flow statement in addition to the information already provided by the income statement and the balance sheet.

We discovered with our look at fixed assets, that the cash amount paid for an asset can be significantly different to the amount charged against profit. In the case of a building, a cash expense of $250,000 payable immediately may result in a charge of $5,000 against the current year profit.

Many forms of income and expense are subject to this type of accounting adjustment. The amount of cash that the business receives and disperses often has no relation to the income statement. The cash flow statement allows us to see 'in real time' how much cash is being generated and how it is being used.

An example of a cash flow statement is shown in Figure Five.

Company Name

Cash Flow Statement

	Period ended December 2025	
Net Income	$ 100,000	(1)
Adjustments to reconcile net income to net cash provided by operating activities:		
Depreciation	10,000	(2)
Amortization	2,000	(3)
Changes in operating assets and liabilities:		
Accounts receivable	(200)	(4)
Inventory	300	(5)
Accounts payable	100	(6)
Net cash provided by operating activities	112,200	(7)
Investing Activities		
Purchase of property, plant & equipment	(50,000)	(9)
Maturing Investment	10,000	(8)
Net cash used in investing activities	(40,000)	(12)
Financing Activities		
Issuance of stock	50,000	(10)
Repayment of long term debt	(5,000)	(11)
Net cash used in financing activities	45,000	(13)
Net change in cash and cash equivalents	117,200	(14)
Cash and cash equivalents at beginning of period	20,000	(15)
Cash and cash equivalents at end of period	**$ 137,000**	(16)

Figure Five

The cash flow statement starts with the company's net income (as it appears on the income statement - marked (1) in the example), and then adds or subtracts all the non-cash movements and accounting adjustments to calculate the change in cash during the period. This net change is applied to the opening cash balance to arrive at the actual cash value held by the company (as shown on the balance sheet).

The first section of the cash flow deals with accounting adjustments, such as depreciation (marked (2)) and amortization (marked (3)). This is followed by a section showing changes in working capital - including changes to accounts receivable, inventory and accounts payable (marked (4) - (6)).

The sub-total at this stage shows the amount of cash generated by the operating activities of the business (marked (7)). This is an important figure as many investors treat cash generated by operations as a substitute measure of performance for those type of companies where accounting adjustments have unduly suppressed net income, but which have strong cash flows.

Another section will show separately the cash used for investing. This section will show amounts spent purchasing investments, amounts realised from maturing investments (marked (8)) and other investing activities such as the acquisition of other businesses. Importantly, the section on investing activities also includes capital expenditures, such as amounts spent on property, plant and equipment (marked (9)).

Whereas some investing activities are discretionary, if a company is to grow and remain profitable capital expenditure is a necessity. Because of this, many investors like to deduct capital expenditures from cash flow from operations in order to arrive at one of their preferred metrics: **Free Cash Flow.**

Free cash flow provides a more realistic measure of the potential of the business to generate cash in the future.

In our example Cash Flow statement, free cash flow is calculated by taking net cash provided by operating activities of $112,200 (marked (7)) and deducting purchase of property, plant and equipment of $50,000 (marked (9)) to give a free cash flow figure of $62,200.

The final section of the cash flow statement shows the amount of cash raised by financing, such as from taking out long-term loans or issuing stock (marked (10)), less any deductions, such as for the re-purchase of stock, or repayment of long-term debt (marked (11)).

Finally these adjustments are combined to reconcile the difference between the cash held at the start of the period and the cash held at the end of the period.

On our example statement we take the net cash provided by operating activities ($112,200 marked (7)), deduct the net cash used in investing activities ($40,000 marked (12)). Then add the net cash raised by financing activities ($45,000 marked (13)). This gives us the overall net change in cash ($117,200 marked (14)), which we can add to the opening cash balance ($20,000 marked (15)) to arrive at the net cash at the end of the period ($137,000 marked (16)).

A business has many choices about how it uses its cash. For example, a company may have the choice between holding cash in the bank, or using the cash to purchase another business. The first of these choices is conservative, the second is aggressive. But there is no impact on the income statement either way. A purchase of a business will simply result in one balance sheet number: Cash; being replaced by another: Investments.

So a cash flow statement isn't just about removing the smoothing effect of accounting adjustments it can give us real insight into the attitude and outlook of the business.

The cash balance available to a business will be affected by changes in the composition of working capital. Consider a business that starts with $10,000 of cash. It buys inventory of $8,000 and sells $2,000 of this inventory on credit for $3,000. In terms of income, the business will disclose $1,000 profit - being the profit generated by selling $2,000 of inventory for $3,000. But in terms of cash, the business that started with $10,000 now only has $2,000 remaining. From the original cash $8,000 has been replaced on the balance sheet by $6,000 of inventory and $3,000 of receivables.

Working capital changes can significantly affect cash balances and also tell us something about the business. If the relative value of debtors has increased that could mean that the business has become lackadaisical about collecting money, or it could be a result of tightening credit in its marketplace - a pointer to rougher times ahead.

We have now completed our exploration of the three main financial reports: the income statement, the balance sheet, and the cash flow statement.

These statements give us a good understanding of how businesses operate. But how should we value them?

That is the biggest question facing any investor. And we shall address it next.

Valuation

Introduction

In essence, an investment is a simple proposition. How much are you prepared to pay now for the promise of a future return that exceeds your original investment?

Three questions arise:

- How much do you get back?
- When do you get it?
- What is the risk that you do not get paid?

Professionals and experienced investors have a number of ways to estimate the value of a share. But let's not get overly technical just yet. To better understand what we are doing, let's think about how we might derive a valuation using common sense.

A Common Sense Approach to Valuation

Investments in stocks return capital in two ways:

- Periodic dividend payments
- A lump sum upon the ultimate sale of the investment

Let's address the issue of dividend payments first. Consider the case of a stock in an imaginary, steady business—let's call it Steadco. This business is never likely to grow beyond its current size, but we expect that it will continue to pay a reliable annual dividend of $6 per share.

The current rate of interest paid by your bank for cash held on deposit is 2%.

What would you pay for a share of Steadco?

The way that we have worded this question is important. We do not care what the market is paying for Steadco. And we do not care how Steadco has been valued by any analyst or academic — whether by calculating price over earnings, modelling discounted cash flow, or by throwing bones in the air to see how they land. We simply need to ask the same question that every other participant in the market is asking: What is Steadco worth to me?

Finding an answer to this question gets to the heart of the art of becoming a successful investor.

If we wanted the same return from Steadco as we were able to achieve from the bank, then Steadco's dividend of $6 would equate to a 2% return, and that would make a share of Steadco worth $300.

But we would be crazy to invest in Steadco for 2% when we could get a risk-free return of 2% from the bank. And that is the crux of the matter — risk.

At a price of $200, Steadco gives us a return of 3% — much better than the bank. But can we risk it?

How about $100? Steadco is now giving us a 6% return, when all those mugs with their money on deposit are only getting 2%! But who will be the mug if Steadco folds tomorrow?

The reality is that nobody knows whether Steadco will plow on steadfastly for many years to come, or whether we will find the financial controller on the front page of the Wall Street Journal tomorrow accused of every fraud under the sun.

We must use our own judgment to value the risk and decide what Steadco is worth.

It is this subjective assessment of risk and return that makes investing such a fascinating and interesting pastime. Very rarely will two individuals completely agree on the "riskiness" of an individual business.

Steadco is a contrived example. A business with a completely steady dividend and zero ongoing growth is unrealistic. When we invest in a business, we hope for capital growth as well as dividend income. Let's consider another imaginary business: Growinc—a high-flying technology company.

Growinc pays no dividends and makes no profits. It plows back all of its earnings into building the business and is currently growing revenues at 40% per year. Growinc's current revenue is equivalent to $100 for every share in circulation.

What would you pay for a share in Growinc?

It's much easier to assign a value to an investment like Steadco, where the return closely resembles that of a cash deposit. Growinc may be growing like crazy—for now (nothing grows forever)—but with no prospect of an immediate return and no firm indication of when that return may occur, how do you decide what the business is worth?

To adapt the approach that we used for Steadco, imagine Growinc as it will be in a few years' time, when the business has stabilized and cash is flowing.

Let's say that we envisage that Growinc will achieve growth of 40%, 30%, 20%, and 10% over the next 5 years. That would give us revenues as follows:

Year 1: $100
Year 2: ($100 × (1 + 40%)) = $140
Year 3: ($140 × (1 + 30%)) = $182
Year 4: ($182 × (1 + 20%)) = $218
Year 5: ($218 × (1 + 10%)) = $240

At this stage, we assume it becomes a steady business with operating returns of 10% per year, or $24 per share.

If we decide that we want a minimum of the 6% return that we achieved for Steadco, then that would value a share of Growinc at ((24 / 6) × 100) = $400 in 5 years' time.

What would we pay now for something that will be worth $400 in 5 years?

Let's assume that the value that we assign to the shares rises in proportion with the growth of the business. In that case, if a business with $240 of sales is worth $400, then a business with $100 of sales is worth ((100 / 240) × 400) = $166.

Let's be clear—you won't find this way of valuing a business in any other textbook or journal. This is not a roundabout way of introducing you to some standard market theory. It's just doing what we said we would do—in the absence of any other information, we are finding a way to value a business using common sense.

You may want to further discount the value of $166 to account for the risk that the growth may not work out as planned. Or you may decide that under your version of common sense, you would value the business totally differently.

Every investment that you consider will have a value based upon a combination of capital growth and income.

We have valued Steadco and Growinc by taking a common-sense approach. The techniques used by investment professionals may seem abstract, but in essence they boil down to finding a way to answer the same questions that we have been faced with here. How do you assess and value the future cash flows that we can expect to get?

The obvious starting point was to compare the investment return with the interest returned from a bank deposit. This is an important point.

The value of stocks depends upon the level of interest rates.

If an investor can get a risk-free return of 8% by investing in U.S. Treasury bonds, then that investor will demand a much higher return from an investment in high-risk stocks. High returns equate to low stock prices. On the other hand, if U.S. Treasuries are paying less than 2%, then a stock dividend of 5% becomes very appealing.

The Professional Approach to Valuation

Discounted Cash Flow

The preferred method used by many professional fund managers and stock analysts to derive a valuation is to perform a **discounted cash flow** analysis (DCF). In practice, few retail investors value their stocks using discounted cash flow.

More importantly, not one of the successful investors studied in composing this book uses DCF as their system for valuing stocks.

Charlie Munger once remarked of Buffett, "Warren often talks about these discounted cash flows, but I've never seen him do one."

You may be wondering at this stage why we choose to study discounted cash flow before any other formal method when we have already established that not one of our involuntary mentors subscribes to it.

It all comes down to how we define the real value of a business. The value of a business derives from its ability to generate a future stream of cash. More specifically:

The value of a business is equal to the present value of all of its future cash flows.

Defining the value of a business and finding a sensible way to assess the value of a business are two different issues (more of the latter later). But by starting from a definition, our approach to valuation will be more critical and better informed. So let's start by getting an understanding of what a DCF analysis is and how it is calculated.

Think about this for a minute. It's quite an elegant concept. By taking the value of all the future cash receipts, we can find a value for the business today. But how can we assign a value to cash that will be received in the future?

Let's use a simple example. Consider a business—let's call it "Two Year Wonder." It has no meaningful assets, but it expects to earn $1,000 next year and $1,500 the following year, at which point it ceases to trade. What is the value of the business?

The value of $1,000 next year is not the same as $1,000 today. We have lost the opportunity of investing that cash for a whole year. And the value of $1,500 two years hence must be discounted even more—we have lost the opportunity of investing that cash for two years.

Let's assume that we are aiming to make 15% on our stock market investments. What is the present value of a future receipt of $1,000 in one year's time? Whatever the value is now, when it has grown by 15%, it will be worth $1,000. To increase an amount by 15%, we multiply by (1 + 15%), which is the same as (1 + (15/100)) or 1.15. So we can say mathematically:

Cash Value Now × (1 + 15%) = $1,000

Therefore:

Cash Value Now = $1,000 / (1 + 15%) = $869.57

Let's use the same technique to work out the cash value now of $1,500 in two years' time. We don't know the cash value now, but we do know that in one year it will be worth 15% more. So we can say:

Cash Value Now × (1 + 15%) = Cash Value In 1 Year

And we know that when a further year has passed, the cash value in that year becomes \$1,500, so we can say:

Cash Value in 1 Year × (1 + 15%) = \$1,500

But we already know that the cash value in one year is the same as (Cash Value Now) × (1 + 15%). So we can substitute the "Cash Value in 1 Year" in the previous equation to get:

(Cash Value Now) × (1 + 15%) × (1 + 15%) = \$1,500

Therefore:

Cash Value Now = \$1,500 / ((1 + 15%) × (1 + 15%)) = \$1,134.22

So we know that the value of \$1,000 in a year's time is \$869.57, and we also know that the value of \$1,500 in two years' time is \$1,134.22. So adding these together, we calculate the value of the "Two Year Wonder" business to be:

\$869.57 + \$1,134.22 = \$2,003.79

Let's make this a little more general so that we can use it more easily in the future. Another way of looking at the return that we demand from an investment is to think of it from the point of view of the business. It is the amount that the business must return to us, the shareholders, in order to access our capital. Thus it is a cost to the business and is generally referred to as the **cost of capital**. We can express our first equation more generally as:

Cash Value Now × (1 + Cost of Capital) = Cash Value In 1 Year

Following the logic of our example above, we can extend this for another year:

Cash Value Now × (1 + Cost of Capital) × (1 + Cost of Capital) = Cash Value In 2 Years

Which is the same as:

Cash Value Now × (1 + Cost of Capital)^2 = Cash Value In 2 Years

For each subsequent year, the Cash Value Now will be increased again by the cost of capital, so we can say that over three years:

Cash Value Now × (1 + Cost of Capital)^3 = Cash Value In 3 Years

We can rearrange this so that we get an expression representing Cash Value Now:

Cash Value Now = Cash Value In 3 Years / (1 + Cost of Capital)^3

We can keep extending this for any number of years into the future. For example, the present value of cash that will be received in 9 years' time is:

Cash Value Now = Cash Value In 9 Years / (1 + Cost of Capital)^9

It is conventional in mathematics to use the letter N for a general unspecified number. So we can say that the present value of cash to be received in N years' time is given by the equation:

Cash Value Now = Cash Value In N Years / (1 + Cost of Capital)^{N}

This is all well and good but not very practical. How can we predict the cash flows of a business for each year into the future until the business ceases to trade?

In reality, we cannot predict each single year into the future with any accuracy, but we might be able to make some sensible, broad assumptions about the average ongoing cash flows and rate of growth.

When we looked at Steadco, we decided upon a value for a steady dividend period forever with no growth and no inflation. In reality, the income of a business tends to grow over time through a combination of organic growth and inflation.

To calculate a value for Steadco based upon its future cash flows, we need to add together the present value of the increasing cash flows for all future years, theoretically stretching into infinity. The value we would assign today to cash that will be received in 20 years' time is clearly quite small, and as the periods stretch far into the future, the value of the receipts for those periods will diminish to a negligible contribution.

Whereas this is easy to understand intuitively, as a practical calculation it involves some tricky mathematics, which, luckily for us, have already been addressed. The equation most commonly used by analysts to value a steadily growing cash stream is the Gordon Growth Model, named after Myron J. Gordon of the University of Toronto. It is:

Current Value($) = Current Cash Flow($) / (Cost of Capital (%) - Rate of Growth (%))

The important things to note about this equation are: (1) A lower cost of capital will result in a higher valuation, and (2) A higher rate of growth will also result in a higher valuation.

This is very similar in concept to the way that we looked at our valuation of Steadco. Then, we asked, "What rate of interest could we get from the bank? How much more would we require in order to take the risk of investing in Steadco?" Under the Gordon Growth Model, we are relating the valuation to the cost of capital to the company, which is equivalent to the rate of return that we are looking for as investors.

Businesses get capital from two sources: by issuing shares or by taking on debt. Shareholders demand a higher return than debt holders. In the case of a business using debt finance, the cost of capital will be a blend of the returns made by shareholders and the rate paid to debt holders. An average value is used, calculated proportionate to the value of shares and debt issued. This is known as the **weighted cost of capital**.

To get a feel for how a discounted cash flow calculation works for a steadily growing business, let's use some specific figures. Let's assume that the investors in a business are looking for a return of ten percent, and the business is expecting steady growth of 5 percent. If this business produced results showing income of $10 per share, we would arrive at a value of:

$$10 / (0.10 - 0.05) = \$200 \text{ per share}$$

If growth was zero, this would reduce to:

$$10 / 0.10 = \$100 \text{ per share}$$

The Gordon Growth model is useful for a company with perpetual, low steady growth. Steadco is an ideal candidate. Steadco has steady income of $6 per share and no growth. It has raised 50% of its capital from shareholders expecting a long-term return of no less than 10% and 50% of its capital from debt holders paid a return of 5%. Steadco's weighted cost of capital will be the average of 5% and 10%, which is 7.5%. On a DCF basis, therefore, Steadco's value is:

$$6 / (0.075 - 0.0) = \$80 \text{ per share}$$

Growinc is a different proposition. We cannot use the Gordon Growth model for Growinc as it does not have steady growth and currently has no earnings.

The way to approach this problem is to calculate the present value of the cash flows produced during the high-growth phase by looking at each year individually. The value of the cash produced during the growth years can then be added to the value of the cash produced at the steady state in order to arrive at a final valuation.

Using our "common sense" method for valuing Growinc, we assumed earnings of $24 per share from year 6 onwards. Let's extend our forecast and say that earnings for years 2 through 5 are $2, $5, $11, $18 before finally reaching $24 in year 6.

To get a DCF valuation for Growinc, we need first to work out the value for years 2–5 separately using the earnings numbers for each year ($2, $5, $11, $18). Using the formula we developed earlier, we get:

$$\text{Year 2 Cash Value Now} = 2 / (1 + 0.10)^2 = \$1.65$$
$$\text{Year 3 Cash Value Now} = 5 / (1 + 0.10)^3 = \$3.76$$
$$\text{Year 4 Cash Value Now} = 11 / (1 + 0.10)^4 = \$7.51$$
$$\text{Year 5 Cash Value Now} = 18 / (1 + 0.10)^5 = \$11.18$$

For year 6 onwards, Growinc is in a steady state, so we can apply the Gordon Growth Model. On the basis that Growinc's weighted cost of capital is the same as for Steadco (7.5%) and no future growth, we can calculate the value in year 6 from the earnings figure of $24:

$$\text{Year 6(+) Value} = 24 / (.075 - 0.00) = \$320$$

We can discount this back to a current value using the same method as for the earnings for years 2 to 5:

$$\text{Year 6(+) Cash Value Now} = 320 / (1 + 0.10)^6 = \$180.63$$

Our final valuation for Growinc will be the sum of all the values from year 2 to 5 plus the year 6 and onwards value:

$$1.65 + 3.76 + 7.51 + 11.18 + 180.63 = \$204.73$$

And there you have it! A final valuation of $204.73 per share.

This is the basic framework for carrying out a discounted cash flow valuation.

Limitations of the Discounted Cash Flow Model

The DCF is a great model in theory, but the business you are invested in resides in the real world.

There are two main issues with DCF calculations.

- It depends entirely on your input assumptions, which will almost certainly be wrong for any significant period into the future
- The model is highly sensitive to inputs causing wide variations in results for quite small differences in the input assumptions

Summary

In the words of Yogi Berra, "It's tough to make predictions, especially about the future."

None of the great investors that we have studied uses a formal discounted cash flow calculation as a basis for valuing a business.

Lynch makes no mention of DCF in his book, neither does Philip Fisher. In fact, only one of the investors we have followed has anything positive to say about discounting future cash flows.

Warren Buffett does not disclose how he values a business, but in his 1994 shareholder letter he writes, "We define intrinsic value as the discounted value of the cash that can be taken out of a business during its remaining life. Anyone calculating intrinsic value necessarily comes up with a highly subjective figure that will change both as estimates of future cash flows are revised and as interest rates move. Despite its fuzziness, however, intrinsic value is all-important and is the only logical way to evaluate the relative attractiveness of investments and businesses."

This may sound like an endorsement of DCF, but Buffett doesn't use detailed DCF models. At the 2009 Berkshire Hathaway annual meeting, he was responding to the question, "What do you think of discounted cash flow (DCF) models?" He replied, "... If you need to use a computer or calculator to figure it out, you shouldn't [buy the investment]. Those types of [situations] fall into the 'too-hard' bucket. It should be obvious. It should shout at you, without all the spreadsheets. We see something better."

Then Munger chipped in, "Some of the worst business decisions I've seen came with detailed analysis. The higher math was false precision. They do that in business schools because they've got to do something."

Buffett then added, "The priesthood has to look like they know more... False precision is totally crazy."

It would seem that Buffett doesn't "do" DCF in a formal, academic way. Although he recognizes that, in theory, the intrinsic value of a business is equal to the discounted value of its future cash flows, he realizes that to attempt to calculate a value by precisely forecasting cash flows is impractical. He relies on pragmatic methods to assess value.

Before we move on, let's summarize the position on DCF:

- The value of a business is equal to the present value of all of its future cash flows.
- Calculating a DCF for a growing company is a multi-step process requiring an estimate of cash flows for several years ahead.
- Some of the figures used to calculate the discounted cash flow are contentious.
- Some of the inputs required may be impossible to assess accurately.
- Small inaccuracies in the initial assumptions may cause wild fluctuations in the result.
- Although precise DCF calculations are often meaningless, it is important to recognize the value of future cash flows in an overall valuation of a business.

The Price Earnings Ratio

The Price Earnings Ratio (**P/E Ratio**) is the single most important metric used to assess the valuation of a business. The P/E ratio is calculated by taking the price of a company's stock and dividing it by the Earnings per Share or **EPS**.

Earnings per Share is calculated by dividing a company's net income by the number of shares.

In contrast to DCF, the P/E ratio is easily accessible and simple to calculate.

When we took a common-sense approach to valuation, we considered a company, Steadco, paying a dividend of $6 per share. We decided to value it at $100—equivalent to a 6% return. The P/E ratio is another variation of this approach.

A business may pass all of its earnings to shareholders as dividends, or it may choose to use its earnings to invest in growth. Investment in growth may be a better choice if it produces superior long-term returns. Because of this, instead of valuing a business by reference to the dividends (as we did with Steadco), the P/E ratio values the business by reference to its Net Income.

In the case of Steadco, where the dividend and the net income are the same, the P/E ratio would be $100 / $6 = 16.67.

A business with net income of $5 per share with a $100 share price would have a P/E of $100 / $5 = 20. And a business with a net income of $10 per share and a $100 share price would have a P/E of $100 / $10 = 10.

It is useful to remember that a business producing a 5% return equates to a P/E of 20, and a business producing a 10% return equates to a P/E of 10.

The long-term average P/E for the S&P 500 is about 16, and the long-term average P/E for the UK FTSE 100 is about 15.

Unlike a DCF analysis, the P/E ratio is a very blunt instrument. It takes no account of growth or business quality. A rapidly growing business that has yet to make a profit will not have a P/E ratio.

But nevertheless, the P/E ratio is the most commonly used metric used to value a business. This is partly because it is easy to calculate, and partly because it is so well understood that analysts feel comfortable mentally factoring in its limitations to adjust for growth or quality.

You may hear comments like "XYZ co has a P/E of 32, but that's OK because it's growing like a weed." Or, "ABC Ltd has a P/E of 24, but I don't mind paying up for such a high-quality business."

In general terms, a P/E of around 10 or below is considered to be good, whereas a P/E of around 20 or more is on the high side for a steady business, and analysts will be looking for a reason to justify the P/E, such as the expectation of growing profits.

Some industry sectors have generally high P/E values, and some have generally low P/E values. For example, restaurants are often thought to have a well-mapped path to growth and are often allowed generous P/E values. Chip manufacturers are thought to be prone to cut-throat competition and commoditization, so are generally given a stingy P/E by the market.

For this reason, you should be wary of making a decision on whether a particular stock looks "cheap" from its P/E until you have made a proper comparison with other players in its market sector.

An often overlooked factor is the influence of interest rates. When we used a common-sense approach to valuing a stock, the question we first asked was "what return can I get from simply putting my money in the bank?"

If you can get a 5% return by investing in government bonds, then you will not be interested in investing in stocks for the same return. But if government bonds are returning 1%, then a 5% return from stocks looks very good.

A stock with a P/E of 20 will be attractive when bond rates are 1%, but when bond rates are at 5%, we may require a P/E of 15 or even 10 for the same business.

When you hear commentators say that "stocks are expensive because the market P/E is a couple of points over its long-term average," always bear in mind that if interest rates are low, stocks are not expensive at all. But if interest rates are high, stocks can still be expensive even when the market has a P/E below its long-term average. Warren Buffett is fond of saying that interest rates act "like gravity" on stock prices.

One of the main issues with the P/E ratio is that it cannot be used to value growing companies as they have little or no earnings. In this instance, another ratio can be useful.

The Price to Sales Ratio

When we tried to use a common-sense approach to value Growinc, we decided to look into the future and attempt to forecast what the earnings would be when the business stabilizes and net profit margins reach a normal level.

If we have a rough idea what the net profit margin is likely to be when the business is stable, we can get an estimate of the likely earnings by applying the net profit margin to the revenue. For example, if we think that revenues will grow by 100% for 2 years from $2.5M today, and then the business will stabilize with net profit margins of 10%, we will reach $10M revenues in 2 years' time ($2.5M × 2 × 2) with forecast earnings of $1M (10% of $10M).

If we want our business today to have an equivalent P/E of 20 on these future earnings, it will have a market value of $20M (if Price over Earnings of $1M is 20, then price must be $20M—"Price" and "Market Value" are identical here because we are dealing with the business as a whole and not a single share).

Looking at today's numbers, we have no earnings, but we do have revenues of $2.5M. We are giving the business a value equivalent to 8 times today's sales.

We can use the ratio of stock price to sales as a yardstick to compare our business with other businesses at the same stage of growth in the same industry. A price to sales ratio less than 8 for a competitive business may be indicative of better value, whereas a price to sales ratio of more than 8 is less attractive.

Of course, we are assuming that businesses at the same stage of development will have the same rate of growth and will end up with the same net profit margins. Consequently, Price to Sales is a very loose tool for valuing a business. If you have enough information and imagination to look forward and get a feel for what the business's P/E will be in the future, that may be a better way to estimate a valuation. But when information and time constraints are limited, the Price to Sales ratio gives you a rough-and-ready way to evaluate and compare growing businesses in the same sector.

Price to Book Ratio

Some businesses are difficult to measure using traditional metrics. Complex financial businesses such as banks or insurance companies are prime examples. This is what Warren Buffett said about banks in his 1990 shareholder letter: "The banking business is no favorite of ours. When assets are twenty times equity—a common ratio in this industry—mistakes that involve only a small portion of assets can destroy a major portion of equity."

The returns made by insurance companies can fluctuate wildly because the level of claims made is unpredictable—depending as it does on the frequency of disasters.

Investors prefer to look at a different metric to assess the value of these types of companies. Instead of focusing on income, they prefer to value the business by looking at its underlying assets—the **book value** of the business.

Those of you who are feeling particularly sharp might be thinking, "Why? Isn't that the same as shareholder equity?" And you would be right. Net Assets, Book Value, and Equity are all the same—it is conventional to use the term book value when discussing valuation.

Conservative investors go further. They like to use **Tangible Book Value**—book value after deducting intangible assets such as goodwill.

The logic behind using book value is based on a liquidation scenario. If the ratio of price to book value is less than one, and the company ceases to trade, the assets liquidated and returned to the shareholders will be greater than the value of the shares. Intangible assets rarely realize value when liquidated, and this is the reason conservative investors prefer to use the narrower figure.

In practice, a liquidation realizes only a fraction of the book value of the assets, and the likelihood of there being any value left for shareholders after paying off liquidation fees and preferred creditors is negligible.

Bear in mind that some very profitable businesses are based upon strong brands and the quality of their people. They will have low tangible book value. Businesses like airlines have a high tangible book value but can be far more risky as they require high levels of capital investment.

Before using tangible book value as an indicator of the quality of a business, think carefully about the type of business.

Banks and insurance companies are well suited to a book value approach, but for most businesses, it is an inappropriate measure.

Before we move on to look at earnings, let's summarize the valuation methods that we have covered:

- The Discounted Cash Flow method (DCF) values a business by calculating the net present value of all future cash flows.
- The Price Earnings Ratio (P/E) measures the relative value of a business in relation to its peers by reference to the ratio of its share price to earnings per share.
- The Price to Sales ratio measures the relative value of a business in relation to its peers by reference to the ratio of its share price to its revenues.
- The Price to Book ratio measures the relative value of a business in relation to its peers by reference to the ratio of its share price to its book value (net assets).

Calculating Earnings for Valuation Purposes

Introduction

We have looked at methods for valuing a business based on future cash flow, the price earnings ratio, the price to sales ratio, and the price to book ratio.

The most common method used to value a business, by far, is the P/E. The method most often used by Wall Street analysts is a discounted cash flow.

Either way, a proper assessment of earnings is essential. And it is earnings that will occupy our attention for most of the rest of this chapter.

Adjusted Earnings

When you look at a company's earnings press release, you will often find that two different measures for income, revenue, or cash flow are quoted. For example, Valeant's press release for the 3rd quarter results 2015 states, "GAAP EPS \$0.14; Cash EPS \$2.74," and later, "GAAP Operating Cash Flow \$737 million... Adjusted Operating Cash Flow \$865 million."

GAAP stands for Generally Accepted Accounting Principles. When companies file their results, they are required to do so following strict accounting rules as determined by the relevant legislation for their place of incorporation. They may also be required to conform with any further requirements demanded by their host stock exchange. Outside the U.S.A. IFRS is used which is very similar to GAAP, (you can assume that when we refer to GAAP this also applies to IFRS for non-U.S.A. companies).

This presents a problem. When you calculate a company's P/E ratio, which earnings figure do you use—the GAAP figures or management's version? You also have an issue of timeframe. Should you use last year's actual results or next year's forecast results? We will look at the matter of timing later. For now, let's consider the matter of earnings.

When GAAP figures are used, you can have confidence that the results have not been distorted by management to present the figures in a more flattering way than would otherwise have been the case.

The company's management will often make the case that GAAP results give a misleading picture of the performance of the underlying business. A company required to amortize intangible assets by GAAP may show a loss, while at the same time operating results are improving and cash flow is increasing. Management will say that the operating results give a much better indication of the health of the business than that presented by GAAP.

In fairness, management does have a point. A business with strong, reliable cash flows and a weak GAAP profit is far more appealing prospect than a business with an apparently healthy GAAP profit but with negative cash flow.

Another reason that management may give for adjusting earnings is to give a better picture of the underlying performance of the business. A growing business may be difficult to evaluate using normal metrics as many of the costs that will be incurred in the early years will dwindle away as the business achieves economies of scale and establishes its reputation. Management adjusts the accounts in an attempt to create a window through which to view the operating performance of the underlying business.

To "help" investors, management will often present an alternative set of results alongside the official GAAP version—usually referred to as **Adjusted Results**.

How are adjusted results calculated? The most important thing to remember is, *there are no rules*.

It has become normal for Wall Street analysts and many financial commentators to use adjusted results for P/E calculations and in discussion on business performance with no acknowledgment that they are basing their assessment on adjusted figures. Often, these adjustments will be for significant amounts.

It is easy to start falling into the trap of treating the adjusted figures as the "normal" figures.

Any analysis based on adjusted figures should be taken with a huge dollop of skepticism. Make a conscious effort to identify the adjustments and understand why it makes sense to use them.

Remember that many businesses are content to report and present their results without resorting to non-GAAP measures.

The most common adjustments made by management are in respect of: depreciation and amortization, stock-based compensation, warrant revaluation, and one-off costs. Let's review each of these in turn.

Depreciation and Amortization

Depreciation and amortization are used to account for the decline in the value of an asset over time. Consider a business that raises capital to start a factory, purchasing plant for $10M. Under GAAP rules, the business would be required to show an expense of $1M each year (assuming that the policy of the business is to depreciate plant over 10 years).

If adjusted earnings, which exclude depreciation, are used, the business will show a profit of $1M more over each of the 10 years—a much rosier picture.

The rub comes in year eleven. The plant is now obsolete, and the business is required to purchase new plant at a price of $15M—a significant and immediate cash outflow. Under GAAP rules, the expense will be taken against profit at $1.5M each year over the next ten years.

The company's adjusted earnings will show a profit that is $1.5M better for each of these next ten years. The $25M of actual cash that has been spent will never show in the adjusted earnings *at all*.

Does it make any sense to base your valuation of the business on figures that ignore this huge outflow of cash?

As ever, the situation is not straightforward. Another business may purchase office property in Manhattan for $10M depreciated under GAAP at $500K per year over 20 years. At the end of the period, the property may be worth $100M —a real gain of $9M per year shown as a loss of $1M on the company's accounts.

Amortization of intellectual property such as brand names will throw up equally quirky results. As a business grows, the value of the brand may increase exponentially while it is being gradually whittled down to nothing on the balance sheet.

Some businesses will produce adjusted results that add back the expense for depreciation and amortization but then deduct the amount required for capital expenditure. This is a much safer approach and gives a much better picture of the true operating performance of the business.

If a company's adjusted figures add back depreciation or amortization, find out why and ask yourself whether the adjustment makes sense. Most assets do depreciate. And even well-known brands decline in value eventually.

Stock-Based Compensation

It is common for companies to compensate employees by issuing them with shares as an alternative to paying them in cash. On the face of it, this seems like an excellent idea.

If employees are happy with share certificates, why use up valuable cash when issuing share certificates costs nothing?

The glaring error here is that issuing shares does not "cost nothing." If a company with 1,000 shares issues another 1,000 as stock-based compensation, then a shareholder with 500 shares will see his ownership of the business reduce from a 50% stake to a 25% stake. Hardly a "nothing" cost to the shareholder!

Analysts will defend this practice by saying that the GAAP practice of deducting stock-based compensation from earnings is "double-counting" because when you calculate the P/E ratio using the diluted share count, the stock-based compensation is already accounted for as the shares issued will be included as diluted shares.

To understand whether this argument has any merit, it is first necessary to deconstruct the process of issuing stock as compensation.

Consider a business that pays its employees salaries in cash to the amount of $1M per year. In the same year, the company decides to raise capital on the market and sells $1M of shares, which are represented in the accounts as an extra $1M in cash and an additional $1M in share capital on the balance sheet.

Would you need to make any adjustment for "double counting" for this business? Certainly not. The accounting for wages as an expense is absolutely standard (debit Wages $1M, credit Cash $1M), as is the practice of recording a capital raise (debit Cash $1M, credit Share Capital $1M).

What if you should now discover that all of the shares issued on the market were purchased by the employees? What is the difference?—None. They are just as entitled to buy shares as anybody else.

Now, take it a step further and let's save some time. Instead of the business paying the employees in cash, and the employees using that cash to purchase shares, why not short-circuit the process and simply issue the shares to the employees?

In terms of accounting, we replace:

> Debit Wages $1M Credit Cash $1M
> Debit Cash $1M Credit Share Capital $1M

with

> Debit Wages $1M Credit Share Capital $1M

But under the first option, the cash transactions canceled each other out. The transactions are identical!

A business that uses stock-based compensation is no different in essence to a business that pays its employees in cash while raising additional capital each year on the market. You would not make any adjustments to the accounts of the latter, so there is no reason whatsoever why you should consider adjusting the accounts of the former.

Stock-based compensation also has the effect of making the accounts less transparent. Consider these two businesses:

Business A Shares: 1,000 Share Price: $1 GAAP Income: $100 Compensation (paid cash): $10 P/E = 10

Business B Shares: 1,000 Share Price: $1 GAAP Income: $100 Compensation (paid as 10 × $1 shares): $10 Diluted Shares: 1010 Adjusted Income (adding back share-based compensation): 110 P/E as adjusted = 1010 / 110 = 9.18

Using the P/E metric, the business using share-based compensation looks to be a better business than the business paying its employees in cash—but in other ways the businesses are identical. It would appear that the business using share-based compensation presents a misleading picture.

Ah, you might say, but if the share price was determined by the industry P/E, then the price would be adjusted by the market to match the P/E, and everything would be brought into balance.

And thus we could get into a circular argument, described rather succinctly by Aswath Damodaran as "a long and tortured road."

Valuation considerations aside, another way to evaluate whether stock-based compensation is a good or a bad thing is to consider a simple scenario. Imagine a business that has 1,000 shares and makes an income of $100 per year. At a P/E of 10, this gives a $1 share price. Each year for 5 years, it pays its employees by awarding them 200 shares—the value of which is reflected fairly in the P&L according to GAAP. At the end of 5 years, the business still makes an income of $100 per year, and the market, quite reasonably, still awards the business a P/E of 10. But there are now 2,000 shares, and the share price is cut in half to 50c.

Warren Buffett puts it like this: "If options aren't a form of compensation, what are they? If compensation isn't an expense, what is it? And if expenses should not go into the calculation of earnings, where in the world should they go?"

Because stock-based compensation is equivalent to raising capital, over time it will cause the amount of shareholder equity to increase sharply, and the business's Return on Equity (ROE) to diminish. This highlights the importance of using a variety of performance metrics. A business that is profligate in the way it raises capital will be identified by its poor ROE rating.

Another issue with stock-based compensation is that it is not always clear what stock has been issued (and therefore included in the share count) and what stock is earmarked for issue in order to satisfy share options that have been granted to management but not yet exercised.

To simplify calculating the P/E, it is easier to ignore the "per share" figures and use the following formula suggested by Aswath Damodaran:

> P/E = (Market capitalization + Estimated value of options outstanding) / GAAP Net Income

Given the problems with stock-based compensation, why does any business use it in the first place?

High-tech companies have established a culture of rewarding highly skilled staff with stock, and they would find recruitment difficult if they did not offer an attractive stock-based package. Stories abound about employees becoming extremely rich as the stock they have received increases exponentially in value. It is a story that potential employees buy into — the Silicon Valley culture.

Companies in high-growth areas are capital hungry. Using stock-based compensation enables them to conserve funds so that they do not have to continually seek further capital in the markets.

Stock-based compensation may not be "shareholder friendly" with regard to the analysis of a business, but there are solid practical reasons for high-growth businesses to use it.

How should you view earnings figures that have been adjusted for stock-based compensation? Simply follow the lead of Warren Buffett and add the figure back.

Warrant Revaluations

A warrant is a financial instrument that gives the buyer the right to purchase stock of a company at some future date at a predetermined price. Warrants are often issued in conjunction with bonds in order to sweeten the deal for the bond purchaser.

Consider a business with shares currently quoted at $100. The business issues $50 warrants at a price of $50, which may be exercised at any time within five years.

Three years later, the company's share price has risen to $200. The warrant holders now have the right to demand their shares for an additional payment of $50. This represents a dilution to the existing shareholders. Issuing an equivalent number of shares on the open market would raise twice the price paid by the warrant holders.

Under GAAP, the company posts an adjustment to the profit and loss account to represent the cost of this dilution. Calculating the amount of the adjustment is not completely straightforward as it has to account for the cost of capital deferred over time. (In practice, this is done using a mathematical model known as the Black-Scholes method).

Fortunately, understanding the precise nature of the calculation is not relevant to us as investors (phew!) as we can rely on the company's auditors to make sure that the job is done properly.

Because warrant revaluations are a non-cash expense, management will usually add back this cost in calculating the adjusted income.

Nonetheless, it is important to realize that this is a real cost to the business.

One-Off Costs

From time to time, a company may incur unexpected or extraordinary expenditure that is not likely to be repeated in the future. For example, the cost of acquiring another business, major litigation expenses, or the costs associated with an unexpected natural disaster.

Because the addition of these costs obscures the normal profitability of the business, management will deduct them in calculating adjusted earnings.

Be wary of the business that adjusts for non-recurring costs on a regular basis. Following the financial crises, many of the banks adjusted their accounts year in, year out for the "one-off" costs of litigation. (Recurring non-recurring costs are not non-recurring!)

Evaluating Operating Performance

Management produces adjusted earnings for two reasons:

- Because GAAP figures are misleading or just plain wrong
- In order to create a window to the underlying operating performance of the business

The first of these reasons presents no challenge to the investor. If an asset is being amortized when in reality it is appreciating, GAAP earnings figures do not present an accurate picture of the business.

In more recent times, adjustments made for the second reason have become more prevalent, and earnings that have been adjusted on this basis present a trap for the unwary investor.

Let's first look at the rationale for creating a window into operating performance. Consider two restaurant businesses. One newly established with heavy debt that is carrying out a thriving, growing trade. The second with a mountain of cash on the balance sheet but with a tired menu and stagnant growth. Because the first business has very high interest costs, its net profits are low. The second business, on the other hand, shows a good net profit margin because it is not saddled with interest payments—on the contrary, it has a little extra income to show from investing its surplus cash.

Wind the clock on a little, and the growing business will have paid off its debt, its business is still growing, and now has lucrative margins. While the second business has further ossified, is losing customers, and its margins are dwindling.

We could have foreseen this better if we had assessed the first business by removing the interest payments from its income statement before comparing the two businesses.

Some expenses can be thought of as normal operating expenses—such as cost of goods sold, salaries, or rent. Other expenses, such as interest payments, taxes, or amortization, can be thought of as disconnected from the core operation of the business.

In order to compare the operating performance of a business, a common measure of performance has emerged: Earnings Before Interest, Taxes, Depreciation, and Amortization—**EBITDA** (usually pronounced as a word rather than a sequence of letters—EBB-IT-DAH).

EBITDA has become so pervasive that it is not only used as an adjustment in isolation—it will frequently be used to replace earnings in calculating a pseudo P/E ratio. You will hear analysts say things like "it's only trading at 12 times EBITDA—so it's cheap."

In fact, it's become so pervasive that many investors fall into the trap of treating EBITDA as a straight replacement for earnings, particularly for companies where there are no earnings.

It is important to remember that expenses like taxes and depreciation are very real, permanent expenses. For the many companies that finance their balance sheet with debt on an ongoing basis, interest expense is not a transient phenomenon. And amortization charges may be perfectly justified.

The picture gets further clouded when we have companies reporting GAAP figures, Adjusted Earnings, and EBITDA alongside each other. Sometimes instead of adjusted earnings, we get adjusted EBITDA. On other occasions, we get adjusted earnings as well as adjusted EBITDA!

The best way to deal with all of this is to follow the intent of management. But do not rely on their calculation of adjusted earnings.

Bringing it All Together

Because there are no rules to the way adjusted earnings are produced, you should decide for yourself whether using adjusted earnings is appropriate and use a consistent method for looking at the various businesses that you evaluate for investment.

In general, GAAP figures should form the foundation of your approach. Any adjustment that you accept should be done after due consideration and for a definite purpose. For the most part, it is not a bad idea to ignore the adjusted figures produced by management until you have followed the business for a few years and have a clear understanding of what message the adjusted earnings convey.

If a business has just made a series of acquisitions or just concluded major litigation, and you wish to form a view of the company's future prospects, it makes sense to look at profit margins after removing the acquisition or litigation expense. But never forget that these are still real expenses.

Warren Buffett makes very few adjustments to GAAP earnings. The important adjustments that he does make are selective and center around amortization. He addressed adjustments in his 2015 shareholder letter as follows:

"I won't explain all of the adjustments—some are tiny and arcane—but serious investors should understand the disparate nature of intangible assets. Some truly deplete in value over time, while others in no way lose value. For software, as a big example, amortization charges are very real expenses. Conversely, the concept of recording charges against other intangibles, such as customer relationships, arises from purchase-accounting rules and clearly does not reflect economic reality. GAAP accounting draws no distinction between the two types of charges. Both, that is, are recorded as expenses when earnings are calculated—even though, from an investor's viewpoint, they could not differ more."

In fact, the only adjustment that Buffett recommends to the individual investor is an adjustment of amortization charges. The following extended quote has been included at length because it gives an authoritative view from the world's greatest investor as to how you should regard adjusted earnings:

"I suggest that you ignore a portion of GAAP amortization costs. But it is with some trepidation that I do that, knowing that it has become common for managers to tell their owners to ignore certain expense items that are all too real. 'Stock-based compensation' is the most egregious example. The very name says it all: 'compensation.' If compensation isn't an expense, what is it? And if real and recurring expenses don't belong in the calculation of earnings, where in the world do they belong?

Wall Street analysts often play their part in this charade, too, parroting the phony, compensation-ignoring 'earnings' figures fed them by managements. Maybe the offending analysts don't know any better. Or maybe they fear losing 'access' to management. Or maybe they are cynical, telling themselves that since everyone else is playing the game, why shouldn't they go along with it. Whatever their reasoning, these analysts are guilty of propagating misleading numbers that can deceive investors.

Depreciation charges are a more complicated subject but are almost always true costs. Certainly they are at Berkshire. I wish we could keep our businesses competitive while spending less than our depreciation charge, but in 51 years I've yet to figure out how to do so. Indeed, the depreciation charge we record in our railroad business falls far short of the capital outlays needed to merely keep the railroad running properly, a mismatch that leads to GAAP earnings that are higher than true economic earnings. (This overstatement of earnings exists at all railroads.) When CEOs or investment bankers tout pre-depreciation figures such as EBITDA as a valuation guide, watch their noses lengthen while they speak."

Forward Figures vs Trailing Figures

P/E figures are normally calculated on a trailing year basis. The accounts figures for the previous four quarters are aggregated in order to calculate the various earnings metrics—usually annotated as TTM (Trailing Twelve Months).

Assessing P/E values for a growth business presents a challenge. If earnings are expected to grow by 50%, an expensive-looking P/E of 30 becomes 20 in a year's time and falls to 13 if the share price remains the same.

For this reason, many analysts and publications quote forward P/E figures instead of, or in addition to, the TTM figures. This is fine as far as it goes, but remember the wise words of Yogi Berra: "It's tough to make predictions, especially about the future."

When comparing P/E numbers between different sources, make sure that you confirm that they have been calculated on a consistent basis.

If you are getting to the serious stage in evaluating a business for investment, don't rely on any published ratios—it is surprising how often they are inaccurate. It only takes a minute or two to work out the major ratios for yourself.

A Way to Use P/E for Growing Companies

We can allow much higher P/E values for growing companies than we would for stagnant businesses. We expect that within a few years, the earnings will catch up with the price. But how should we judge how much of an allowance is reasonable?

Peter Lynch writes, "If the P/E of Coca-Cola is 15, you'd expect the company to be growing at about 15 percent a year, etc. But if the P/E ratio is less than the growth rate, you may have found yourself a bargain."

Dividing the P/E ratio by the percentage growth rate is known as the **PEG** ratio.

Following Lynch's criteria, anything with a PEG less than 1 is "a bargain."

The PEG ratio is a quick and convenient way to assess whether a P/E ratio is reasonable in comparison to the growth rate. In general, a PEG ratio greater than 2 is expensive, and a PEG ratio less than 1 is attractive.

The major difficulty in the approach is pegging down the growth rate (pun intentional — sorry).

You can assess the growth rate over the past few years by looking at the financial statements. But as Lynch himself writes, "As to the all-important future growth rate, your guess is as good as mine."

The best an investor can do is to read management's guidance, listen to the conference calls (if they exist), and form a reasonably conservative opinion.

If a company has a consistent operating margin, then you may calculate the growth rate by looking at operating income. But if a young growing company is gradually moving into profitability, this can be misleading, and it is safer to look at the revenue numbers.

An often overlooked issue with the PEG ratio is the significance of the P/E. A company with a high P/E will produce much better returns over a period than a company with the same PEG ratio but a low P/E. Companies with high P/E ratios and low PEG ratios are therefore particularly attractive. Identifying businesses like these was a major contributing factor to Lynch's success.

On the other hand, high-growth companies are much less able to sustain their growth over time. Growing earnings by 10% or even 20% a year over a decade may be possible, but sustained growth of 30% or 40% is much more difficult to achieve.

Final Thoughts on Valuation

For most of this chapter, we have concentrated on finding ways to value companies "by the numbers." Back in 1934, Benjamin Graham published 'Security Analysis'—the indispensable bible at the time for analysts wishing to value stocks on a purely quantitative basis. Graham advised that you should invest in businesses holding assets that exceeded their market value by a minimum "margin of safety." Many intrepid investors made their fortunes by wading through hundreds of annual reports to find stocks that were undervalued. By investing in those with large "margins of safety," many fortunes were made. In his early years, Warren Buffett used this approach to great effect.

In modern times, where computers are pervasive and Wall Street employs hundreds of analysts to crunch the numbers on thousands of listed stocks, it is not possible for an investor to discover a stock that is significantly undervalued on an analytical basis just because it has been overlooked by everyone else.

If you try to find success as a small investor by "doing the math" better than the rest of the market, you will quickly run into trouble. Yes, you should be asking yourself questions like: Does it have a reasonable P/E? Is the PEG reasonable for its rate of growth? If not, can the value be justified on a DCF basis? But these questions should be with an end to having a better understanding of the type of business—another "check in the box" as you make sure there are no untoward red flags.

Wall Street is preoccupied by numbers and short-term thinking. And this is a situation we can turn to our advantage. As Lynch states in his mildly colorful way, "Nothing has occurred to shake my conviction that the typical amateur has advantages over the typical professional fund jockey."

All of the great investors employ a "business first" approach. In chapter five, we took a "deep dive" into the qualities that the best companies possess, and in chapter six, we considered the importance of seeing a viable future for the business—a story that makes sense—or as the professionals would put it, an investment thesis.

It is easy to get bogged down analyzing cash flows, calculating margins, and figuring out P/E ratios — whether forward, backward, adjusted, or double discounted by the exchange rate of the Japanese yen to the Big Mac...

You do need to understand financial statements and valuation techniques. But don't lose sight of the fact that understanding businesses and where they are going is by far the most important part of being a successful investor.

By looking for quality businesses with great management that eschews pandering to the market in the short term, you can outperform professional investors who are inhibited by their straitjacket thinking.

Stocks like Amazon or Facebook have always seemed overvalued by normal market standards, but in hindsight it appears they were dramatically undervalued in relation to their prospects.

Focus on the qualities that make a business great — those qualities that cannot be measured numerically — and you will find real value in the stock market.

Assessing Risk

Introduction

An investor has two main priorities

- Return on capital
- Preservation of capital

It is natural that for most of the time we concentrate on returns. The great investors are optimists, and to become a great investor an optimistic outlook is essential. Otherwise you will always be afraid to take the risks that are necessary in order to achieve great returns.

It is a common mis-conception that entrepreneurs like to take risks. In reality the opposite is true. Entrepreneurs may be forced to take on some risk in order to fulfil their goal, but they do everything they can to avoid taking on any further risk, and are meticulous in doing so.

Similarly, great investors are prepared to make bold moves in seeking out returns. But they are also careful to put a risk management strategy in place to reduce the chance of suffering the investor's worst nightmare - a significant, permanent loss of capital.

Some academics equate risk with volatility or stock Beta[4]. This is not a view shared by the successful investors that we have studied, and the whole idea has been pooh-poohed explicitly by Warren Buffett, 'we define risk, using dictionary terms, as "the possibility of loss or injury"'.

As investors, when we talk about risk it is important to make a distinction between the risk of a major capital loss and the possibility that an investment may suffer a downturn. It is to be accepted that some investments will return more than others, and, unfortunately, some will result in a loss. When we assess a business as a candidate for investment, this possibility is already taken into account.

But when we make a risk assessment of a business, we are not thinking about how a business will perform if it is successful, we are thinking about the likelihood that it will suffer a catastrophic failure. This is an entirely different perspective. And as such, it should be undertaken as a separate process.

Portfolio Risk

In a diversified portfolio, a total loss of a single investment should not be a disaster. Most investors will suffer this from time to time. But if you are not

---

[4] As covered previously under Discounted Cash Flow, the Beta of a stock is the percentage value by which a stock price changes in proportion to a percentage change in the general market.

careful, you may end up with a succession of these events, and that could wreak havoc upon your future.

If your portfolio consists entirely of speculative bio-tech stocks, there is a strong possibility that you may get wiped out. But if all the bets come off… Oo la la. On the other hand if your portfolio is all steady blue-chip stocks you are extremely unlikely to suffer significant loss, but on the other hand you will not get great returns either.

When you are building a portfolio you need to be cognisant of the risks involved with each investment and balance the portfolio accordingly. A large proportion of 'shoot for the moon' investments could end up making you rich, but is just as likely to make you bankrupt.

Before committing to an investment you should ask, 'What is the chance that I could permanently lose a significant majority of my capital?'. If the probability is high, you should be looking for exceptional returns and only be willing to allocate a small proportion of your portfolio.

The much respected investor, Tom Engle, who has contributed regularly to the 'Motley Fool' says, 'If a company is the next big thing, a little position is all I need. If it isn't the next big thing, a little position is all I want'.

If you are investing over a period of decades, regularly allocating a small portion of your portfolio to high risk investments will give you many chances to 'hit the jackpot' with a high return, but will never expose your portfolio as a whole to an unexpected major loss.

Portfolios that produce good returns have a high proportion of moderately risky stocks. Think of names like Amazon, Google, Facebook, Apple, Tesla. Owning these stocks over the years has made many people wealthy. So to be a successful investor you must be prepared to embrace a certain amount of calculated risk.

How you balance your portfolio between high risk, moderate risk, and low risk stocks is a reflection of your personality, and something you must decide for yourself.

Leverage

It can be tempting to use leverage to juice your returns. For example if you have $1,000 to invest, why not borrow a little and buy $2,000 of stocks so that if you get a 10% return it becomes $200 instead of $100?

Many brokers will allow you to do this using **Margin** - which is the amount the broker will lend you using your existing stocks as collateral.

You can also gain leverage using options (which we will discuss in detail later). By buying a call option in a stock you can get all of the upside but at a fraction of the cost.

The problem with leverage is that as much as returns are magnified when things are going well, they can also be magnified catastrophically when things turn south.

The call options that you were convinced would go to the moon suddenly become worthless, your margin is insufficient and you are forced to sell stocks at the worst possible time in order to pay off your debts. And in the worst case scenario you can be wiped out completely.

Remember that nobody knows what the market is going to do in the short term, and as Keynes is supposed to have observed, "The market can remain irrational longer than you can remain solvent."

Do not succumb to the attraction of leverage. It is difficult enough to manage risk without bringing it upon yourself.

There are countless stories of investors having tens of millions of dollars who went on to lose it all through becoming greedy with leverage.

Individual Investment Risks

Risks to individual investments can be thought of as being in two main categories - major risk and cumulative risk.

Major Risk

A major risk arises from a single event or failure that could prove fatal to the prospects of the business. For example:

- A business relying on patent royalties might be challenged in the courts and the patent rendered worthless.
- An industry could be disrupted by a new technology - such as the wholesale change from photographic film to digital cameras that bankrupted Kodak.

Risks like these may or may not be easy to foresee, and there is no easy rule to apply, other than always to be diligent to the commercial context in which any business operates.

A business subject to a clear and obvious major risk should be treated with caution.

Cumulative Risk

Failures caused by a major threat can be spectacular and dramatic. But the more usual reason that a business suddenly hits the skids is more mundane. It may simply run out of money.

Failure may not be attributable to any single factor, but through an accumulation of problems that in the end become too much and overwhelm the business.

Cumulative risks fall into two major categories. Market Risk and Business Risk.

Market Risk

Market risk arises from the way the investment is perceived by the marketplace. It has two main components, Price and Liquidity.

Price

Great businesses do not always make great investments. If a stock has been given a high value by the market, you must have confidence that the business will grow into the valuation. Stocks that are particularly prone to pricing risk, are those subject to hype - such as AI, Robotics, or Biotech. Stocks in nascent industries often follow the Gartner Hype Cycle, shown in Figure Six.

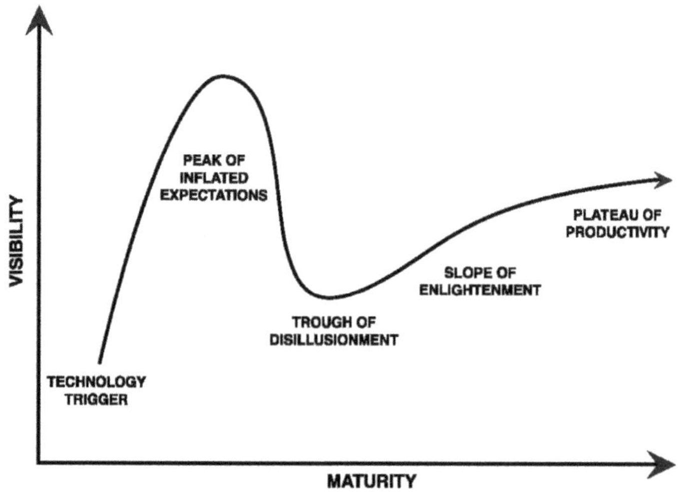

Figure Six

When the technology is new, the market gets excited and has unreasonable short-term expectations. The stock price rockets up, often to silly levels where the price represents hundreds of times the forecast earnings. When it becomes apparent that the short term prospects have been over-hyped, depression sets in and the stock price tumbles.

Gradually, as the fruits of the technology are finally realized the business prospers and the stock rises again, this time in a far more measured way, better reflecting the true value of the business.

Buying stocks that are at the peak of inflated expectations can be a sobering experience, often leading to a 90% loss within a few months.

If the business fails to realize its original expectations, this loss will become permanent.

Then again, if you had ignored fast growing volatile stocks over the last decade, you would have missed out on some of the best investments ever made. Amazon and Facebook both rocketed early only to be hammered by the market later. If you had held these through thick and thin, you would still have made multiples on your original investment, even if you had bought at the peak.

Knowing whether you are at the peak of the hype cycle, or just at the beginning of a fantastic, growing business is easy to see with hindsight, but a lot less clear at the time.

Whether or not you invest in these type of stocks will depend on your own personality, and how you approach risk (more on this later). Warren Buffett has always avoided high-risk, high-growth, technology stocks. But many other successful investors have had great success with them.

If you do elect to operate in this arena, it is important to be aware of the hype cycle and assess the risk accordingly. Many skilled investors will start with a small stake, and get a little 'skin in the game'. You can then add at better value points over time as the story plays out.

Liquidity

Liquidity is a measure of the ease with which you can convert your investment into cash. A house is an illiquid investment - to cash it in requires a potentially long and fraught process as you search for a buyer. A block of stock in IBM is a highly liquid investment - you can convert it into cash instantly whenever the market is open in New York (or even outside market hours if your broker offers this facility).

Be wary of investments offered by finance houses that do not have guaranteed liquidity. Investors in high profile hedge funds have been unpleasantly surprised in recent years to find that they have been unable to withdraw cash as the fund has been unable to realize some of their more illiquid investments.

Stocks with listings on major exchanges will always have high liquidity. Just because a stock is listed for trading by a broker does not guarantee liquidity. Orders placed for stocks traded on the 'pink sheets[5]' may take days to process and often have large bid-ask spreads (the bid-ask spread is the difference in price between the buyer and the seller, which gives the broker his margin. The ask price is the lowest price a seller will accept and the bid price is the highest price a buyer will pay.).

Business Risk

Types of Business Risk

You may come across businesses with sexy technology, charismatic management and a slick PR department painting an inviting picture of great times ahead. It is easy to get swept away by the story. But before committing capital, it is wise to form a more objective opinion as to whether a business is likely to fail.

We will deal with each area of business risk in turn.

---

[5] Stocks on the 'Pink Sheets' are over the counter securities not quoted on a major exchange. They do not need to meet minimum requirements or file with the SEC

Cash

The most important indicator of health in a business is positive cash flow.

A history of positive cash flow over a few years is better, and growing positive cash flow is better still.

Although cash flow is king, be aware that businesses have techniques at their disposal to artificially boost cash flow in the short term to the detriment of the long-term. They can improve their cash flow by re-arranging their balance sheet - through improved debt collection, or by stringing out their suppliers. These improvements are not sustainable. Another ruse is to scale back on capital expenditure or research and development. These are false economies that will hurt the long-term competitiveness of the business.

Often with a young business, the main concern is not cash flow but **cash burn**. The business will be going through cash like crazy as it invests to build a foothold in the marketplace. For these businesses the amount of cash on the balance sheet is the most significant issue.

Established businesses may also go through transitional periods when they must navigate a trough between periods of profitability. For example, a technology business may need to upgrade its products from one platform to another, such as migrating phones from 3G to 4G to 5G. Another example would be a food business like Chipotle Mexican Grill having to deal with a temporary setback caused by a health scare.

For businesses facing short term difficulties, having enough cash to weather the short term storm is vital. Young, growing businesses often underestimate the effort required to become established. Transitions may take longer than anticipated. And sometimes regaining the trust of the public after a health scare takes a while longer than expected.

Businesses with a mountain of cash at hand have the flexibility to navigate their way to calmer waters, whereas the business with limited cash is unlikely to survive the journey.

Profitability

As we have discovered earlier, cash flow does not always equate to profit and vice versa.

Cash flow is a measure of what the business receives today - whereas profit is an attempt to record a fair value of the income generated by a business over time by spreading the cost of capital expenditures and other one-off costs in an even way.

Both are equally important. From a risk point of view we want to see a business that is not only profitable today, but has shown consistent, growing profitability.

GAAP profits offer more comfort than the adjusted figures, which are prone to reflect management's optimism. Risk is about caution.

Revenues

It is possible for a business to show increasing short term profits and cash flows by focussing on cutting costs and reallocating resources to high margin activities.

A better bottom line is always welcome, but in order to achieve consistent future growth, the business must grow its revenues.

When assessing risk, stagnant or declining revenues may be the first sign of troubling times ahead.

Debt

The best protection for a company that runs into unexpected trouble is a pile of cash.

As a fallback position the company may survive troubling times by taking out borrowings. If a business is already saddled with high debt, this option is not available and survival becomes more difficult.

A business saddled with high debt will also face pressing demands from nervous creditors at the first sign of trouble. This in itself can cause instability and end up in a spiralling descent of additional problems as other creditors become more and more nervous as the company's liquidity dries up.

Businesses with high levels of debt to equity may produce great returns for shareholders when times are good, but this may come at the expense of catastrophic failure when things get tough.

Management Capability

A growing business with an entrepreneur at the helm has an intoxicating allure.

But as the business matures the demands of an efficient organization call for different skills to those required for a start-up. Administration, human resource management, accounting, inventory control and order processing are all essential for a maturing business, but to a tech entrepreneur they all sound like boring, boring, boring, boring…

On the other hand, how does a management team that has been running a business in the same way for thirty years respond to a young, fresh upstart?

Inexperience and too many years in the job are both sources of risk.

When Steve Jobs asked John Sculley to run Apple it was for all the right reasons - to bring the steady management hand that the young entrepreneur needed. But in the end that move cost Jobs his position in the company.

Sculley struggled, but it was his management at a time of crises that saved Apple from bankruptcy. Yet, later on it was Sculley's inability to run an entrepreneurial company that stifled Apple's progress, and it was only when the, now more mature, Jobs regained stewardship of the company that Apple really took off.

All of this illustrates why there are no easy answers and why investing can be such a fascinating pastime.

The take-away? A business which does not have a balanced management team with the right blend of flair and experience can quickly run into trouble when times get difficult.

Shareholder Alignment

It is not uncommon to see a charismatic, high profile CEO grow a business spectacularly, inspire adoring followers, and command a super-high salary.

But if the CEO is remunerated by salary alone, there is a significant risk that he or she may be tempted to move to another business offering a better package. The loss of such a charismatic figure could result in significant damage to the business.

Management can only be properly aligned with the interests of share holders if they have a significant portion of their personal wealth tied up in the business. It is also important that the major part of the remuneration that management receives derives from an increasing stock value.

For a growing startup, this could be as much as 50%, or more. For large public companies with a multi-billion pound capitalization, a relatively small percentage holding may still equate to a large percentage of the personal wealth of the firm's management.

Disruptive Competition

Some of the most catastrophic, unexpected failures in business have been caused by disruption from an upstart competitor with a new way of doing things.

Kodak is the classic example, but there are many others. In 'The Innovator's Dilemma' Christensen gives examples in numerous industries where entrenched leaders have suffered catastrophic disruption, including industries as diverse as hydraulic excavators and disk drives.

Unwelcome competition can also be a risk to the disruptor. A large competitor may become aware of a young upstart, and decide to squash it by driving it out of business before it gains momentum.

Branding

We often hear people talk of 'hoovering the carpet' or 'googling the answer'. What better testament to the power of a brand?

Looking from a risk perspective, we can turn the issue on its head and ask, 'But what if a business has no brand?'

If I walk into a supermarket in London to buy chocolate, if I see 'Cadbury' I will pick it up, because I know I can rely upon it. But if there were no recognisable brand names, it would be a random choice.

A company with no brand, has no loyal customer base, and is much more susceptible to competition - a significant risk factor.

There is also a risk that the power of a brand has waned. People may still talk of buying a 'Hoover', when they actually intend to buy a vacuum cleaner from another manufacturer.

Diversified customer base

If a company relies on just a few customers for a large proportion of its sales, the loss of these customers will have a catastrophic effect on the business.

There is a caveat to this risk. Some businesses distribute their product through a small number of wholesalers. If the number of end customers is large and diverse, then reaching the market through a small number of wholesalers would not be a risk factor (unless the wholesaler has significant influence over which products are chosen by retailers).

Using a wholesale organization for fulfilment can actually reduce risk for young growing businesses as it removes the logistical headache of distribution

Transparent financial statements

We judge potential companies for investment on many criteria, but the most significant factor is the financial performance of the business.

Most businesses are fairly easy to understand. They make things or buy things, and they sell things or services.

Some businesses can be very difficult to understand. Banks are a prime example. Before the financial crises of 2008, many banks were thought to have strong balance sheets. As it turned out, those assets turned to dust overnight.

Warren Buffett and Charlie Munger have what they call a 'Too Hard Pile'. Munger said, 'If something is too hard we move on to something else. What could be simpler than that?'.

If there is any difficulty in evaluating the financial statements of a business there is a significant risk that the value imputed to that business is wrong. Do not invest in businesses that you do not understand. If it's too difficult for Warren Buffett, then it's probably too difficult for you.

Risk Evaluation - A Summary

When you think about risk it is important for you to take a pause mentally and put a different cap on.

Good investors approach a business optimistically and look for positive things. That is the way to find businesses that deliver superior returns.

But when we consider risk, we are looking to guard against a significant, permanent loss of capital, and that requires a negative, sceptical outlook. If that seems contradictory, remember the words of F Scott Fitzgerald, 'The test of a first-rate intelligence is the ability to hold two opposed ideas in mind at the same time and still retain the ability to function'.

All businesses have some degree of risk. After all, without risk the market would not give us any reward.

Risk falls into two categories: major risk and cumulative risk.

Major risks should be evaluated and dealt with as separate issues.

Cumulative risk is less obvious, but can be assessed by evaluating a business across a range of market risks and business risks. The level of risk to the business increases as the number of red flags rises.

A young company may have an inexperienced management team, or high debt levels, or a concentrated customer base, or opaque financial statements. But if it has all four? Then it is time to get worried.

When you consider a business for investment, put some time aside to carry out a separate risk analysis. Make a list of all the various factors that we have described above and decide whether the company gets a pass or fail.

Once a business is in your portfolio, any material change to the operating environment of the business - such as a change of management, or increased competition in the marketplace - will have an impact on your investment case. Make sure that you include a risk analysis as part of your reappraisal.

In reality, risks are not equal and there is no absolute rule that determines whether you should invest or stay away. But the results of your risk analysis should be hugely influential in informing your decision.

Every business has risks, and if you are not prepared to take on some level of risk you will be faced with a lifetime of receiving the miserable rewards returned by a bank deposit account.

The trick is to be able to judge when the risk involved in an investment reaches that tipping point when it becomes unacceptable. And, as ever, this depends on developing a good business knowledge.

Buffett says, ‘Overall we’ve done better by avoiding dragons than by slaying them’.

But this is the same Buffett that made a fortune investing in American Express at the height of the Salad Oil scandal.

There is no right or wrong answer with risk. Your tipping point will not be the same as mine or anyone else’s.

It becomes easier to evaluate risk when you have a deep understanding of the business. Peter Lynch really liked to get to know a business close up.

Which takes us neatly on to our next chapter.

Getting to know you….

Getting to Know All About You

In the last few chapters we have concentrated on viewing a business analytically.

But companies are run be people and sometimes the important things can not be measured by numbers alone.

Businesses produce annual reports in which they extol their virtues.

Executives sometimes write articles for the press, or better still give interviews on the radio or television.

In the U.S.A. most businesses give quarterly earnings conference calls where they set out their results and then take questions from analysts.

Back in the 1980s, one of the most significant findings of Tom Peterson and Bob Waterman's book, 'In Search of Excellence' was that culture is far more important than structure. Or in their words, 'The rational model causes us to denigrate the importance of values'.

The attitudes and values of a business should be apparent in all its dealings, whether through interaction with its customers, how it describes itself in the annual report, or the words of the CEO when taking questions on a conference call.

The experience you get when you place an order with Amazon, reflects a business that does everything it can to nurture its customers. It knows your likes and suggests products. It makes the ordering process easy, and despatches items promptly. If there is a problem, it makes it easy for you to make a return and will give a no-quibble rebate.

In the 2015 shareholder letter, Jeff Bezos notes that, although Amazon's retail and web services businesses are completely different on one level, 'They share a distinctive organizational culture that cares deeply about and acts with conviction on a small number of principles. I'm talking about customer obsession rather than competitor obsession, eagerness to invent and pioneer, willingness to fail, the patience to think long-term, and the taking of professional pride in operational excellence'.

That phrase *customer obsession* says it all. Amazon has a distinctive culture and a basic set of values that are unchanging.

That doesn't mean these are the values that every business should have. As Bezos himself says, 'We never claim that our approach is the right one – just that it's ours'.

The most impressive thing about Amazon is not their culture - it's the way that they have adhered to it over the long-term. To reinforce that they include a copy of their 1997 shareholder letter with each new, annual letter. Explaining their approach back then, they state 'We will continue to focus relentlessly on our customers'.

Amazon has not been a straightforward investment for shareholders with wild swings in both directions along the way. But the many investors who have stuck with the company over the years have been richly rewarded. These investors were not focussing on earnings or share price quarter by quarter, they were focussing on the values Bezos believes in. And by listening and reading carefully over the years, they have become comfortable with the consistent message and bought into the vision.

The human brain is not well suited to investing. It is programmed to fight or flee, and it is easy to succumb to the temptation for panic buying or selling when unexpected news comes our way.

By getting to know a business well, you develop a deeper understanding of its leaders, its culture and its values. You get to know their idiosyncrasies and follow the nuances. You know when they are under-promising, and can detect when they become brash.

If you think all this seems soft and irrelevant, and prefer to concentrate on hard numbers, think again. Wall Street is full of analysts that have access to more data than you can imagine. And they have computers that can crunch numbers in nanoseconds. You will not beat them at that game.

What Wall Street is not very good at is recognising businesses that are undervalued through an under-appreciation of their soft qualities - such as culture, leadership and vision.

As a small investor with the luxury of longer timescale and the ability to factor in the advantages of these softer qualities, you have a tremendous edge over the short-term, data-driven Wall Street analyst.

Get to know your investments over time. Read the annual reports, read the shareholder letters, listen to the conference calls.

Many talented CEOs have not got the best public presence. Elon Musk - the Tesla and SpaceX CEO - is controversial in many ways, yet at the same time one of the most talented, visionary leaders that have ever existed.

In his early days, when he spoke he came across as hesitant and unsure. He often turned up at earnings conference calls tired and tetchy, with the result that analysts were unimpressed and the stock price fell.

But having followed Elon, quarter after quarter, and listened to him speak to the media and various public conferences over the years, you learn to see through his moods and the controversy and pick up on what is important - which often might be a leak about some great new product or idea.

Another overlooked advantage of knowing a business well is that you can detect when confidence is shaky and tougher times may loom. At times like these it is important to remember that when the fundamentals of a business begin to turn, then that is the time to exit an investment. It can be difficult sometimes to let go of an investment when you have stuck with it over the years but just as it is important to hold patiently over the years when your investment thesis is intact, it is also important not to let misplaced loyalty prevent you from letting an investment go when the investment thesis becomes broken. Hold on tightly, let go lightly.

Get to know your businesses, it will serve you well.

Derivatives

The Dark Side of the Force?

Many novice investors are intimidated by derivatives. They hear experienced investors discussing them in a language they don't understand and think of them as complicated and risky.

In 'One Up on Wall Street' Peter Lynch writes, 'I've never bought a future nor an option in my entire investing career and I can't imagine buying one now'.

Warren Buffett said, 'In my view, derivatives are financial weapons of mass destruction'.

Bearing these comments in mind, I wouldn't blame you if you stopped reading this chapter here and skipped on to safer ground. But I think that every investor should at least have a basic understanding of derivatives. In some limited cases they can be useful tools for even the most conservative investor.

If you think I've gone off my trolley by disagreeing with Buffett and Lynch, take note that Buffett may have cast his disdain on derivatives, but he does place trades in the derivative market himself. And the options trades used by many modern investors are often used to curtail risk, rather than make the excessive gambles that Lynch describes in his book.

The term derivative as used in the financial world is used to describe a transaction based on an underlying asset. The underlying asset may be a currency, a stock, or a bond or indeed any financial asset that some intrepid financier is prepared to use to make a market.

A derivative can usually be thought of as some kind of bet. 'I bet that shares in IBM will go down by next month' or 'I bet that the pound will increase in value against the dollar by next week'.

As this book is based upon investing in stocks, we shall confine ourselves here to considering the three types of derivative most commonly used in the stock market, Futures, Options and Shorts.

Futures

A futures contract is just like any other form of contract except that the delivery date is at some point in the future. Let's say that IBM shares trade at $150 today, but you expect them to be $200 this time next year. You may be offered the chance to buy IBM 1 year from today at a price of $160, so you could make a potential profit of $40. Not only that, but you have use of your capital for a further year while you wait.

This sounds great, but what if IBM shares fall, say to $140? If you had simply owned the shares you would be down $10, but now you are forced to pay $160 for a $140 share. Furthermore, it is unlikely that your broker will allow you credit on the full $160, so you may be required to put a percentage on deposit.

As the price of IBM stock falls you may be repeatedly asked to add funds to cover your allowed margin[6]. It may not sound such a rosy deal now.

Futures contracts can be useful in some circumstances. Companies that trade cross-border need consistency in pricing in order to know whether they will make a profit. A company trading in New York may be buying beef from Brazil and selling it to a customer in Singapore. The business knows that it will need to pay the Brazilian farmer in Reals in a month's time and will receive Singapore dollars in two months' time. By buying Reals and selling Singapore dollars in the futures market today the business can accurately forecast the profit on the trade. If it could not trade ahead a movement in the currency rates may turn a profitable trade into a loss.

In the stock market, futures trades are more often made on stock indices[7] rather than individual stocks. Sophisticated investors may place future contracts as hedges in order to mitigate risk[8].

If you are investing for the long-term, any short-term hedge has a cost, and this will detract from your total returns. Replying to a question on hedged investment funds Warren Buffett comments, 'Many will sell you the idea of the day. No great statistical merit'. And Charlie Munger adds, 'We made our money by being long wonderful businesses, not by using a long-short strategy'.

None of the successful investors that we have studied use hedging on stock-based portfolios.

Once the element of risk-management is removed, trading in the futures market on stock indices is more like gambling than investing.

When you invest in individual stocks, it is useful to be aware of the futures market, but leave the trading to the gamblers and the speculators.

---

[6] A stock broker may allow you to become overdrawn or take on future liabilities without having sufficient cash in your account to cover them. The amount of overdraft plus liability that you are allowed is your margin. The securities held in your account act as collateral. As prices fluctuate in the market, the amount of your future liabilities may increase, and your collateral may become insufficient to cover your allowed margin, in which case your broker will demand cash to cover the position.

[7] A stock index is a figure calculated by combining the values of a number of stocks which meet pre-set criteria. For example the Dow Jones Industrial Average, the S&P500, the Nasdaq Composite or the FTSE100 are all stock indices.

[8] A hedge is a small position placed in opposition the the general strategy of your overall portfolio. The purpose of a hedge is to mitigate losses if things don't work out as planned. The downside of a hedge is that if things do go as planned, your overall returns will be reduced by the cost of the hedge trade.

Shorts

A **Short** is a transaction where you sell a stock that you do not own, with the intention of buying it back in the future at a lower price.

Shorts are one of the most confusing trades for novice investors to understand. How can you sell a stock that you do not own? You could think about it like an overdraft - how can you spend money that you do not have? By arranging an overdraft, the bank will let you spend the money and charge you interest for the privilege.

Selling stocks short works in a similar way. Your broker will 'lend' you the stock to sell, but will charge you interest on the value of the stock. The broker must then borrow the stock from another holder or another broker. Brokers are given some leeway in balancing short sales against borrowed stock in order to allow the market to function efficiently.

If you hold a stock valued at $10, then the worst thing that can happen is that you lose the whole $10. If you short sell a stock with a value of $10, and that stock then rises in value to $100, you have lost ten times as much as your potential gain. Short selling is expensive, and carries huge risk. Warren Buffett does not short sell stocks. When asked about short selling he replied, 'It's ruined a lot of people. You can go broke doing it'. And as we covered above, Peter Lynch has never shorted a stock.

Short sellers claim to provide a service to the market by discovering scandals like Enron. While this can be true on occasion, it is also true that short selling can be a very grubby profession. Some firms short stocks before embarking on a tirade of media coverage, publishing articles slinging mud at the company that they have just shorted. Retail investors flee in fear, while the short sellers smugly pocket the proceeds.

By the time the hapless retail investors realize that they have been taken for a ride, it is too late to recover their losses and the short sellers have moved on to the next scam. Do not allow yourself to be scared out of a good stock by an unscrupulous short attack.

Options

Options are similar to futures, with one important difference. With a futures contract you undertake to buy or sell a stock at some future date. With an options contract you have the option to buy or sell the stock at a future date, but you are not obligated to do so.

Like other forms of derivatives, options can be extremely risky and dangerous. But they can also serve a useful purpose when employed cautiously.

There are two types of options - **Call** options and **Put** options.

Call Options

Ownership of a Call option gives you the right to purchase a stock at a fixed price at any time before a fixed date[9]. Stock XXX trades at $10. You purchase a call option for $6 that gives you the right to buy the stock for $5 in a year's time.

In effect, you are paying $11 for a $10 stock ($6 today and $5 in a year). Why would you do this?

Let's say that you expect the price of the stock to rise to $15. If you had purchased the stock normally at the market price of $10, you would make a return of 50%. But if you purchase the call option, you make a gain of $4 ($15 - $11) on a capital outlay of $6 . That's a gain of 66% - a 16% improvement. (In order to realize this gain, you would need to immediately sell the stock for $15.)

The downside is that if the stock goes to $10.50, when you exercise your option you are left with a loss of 50c ($10.50 - $11), whereas a holder of the stock would have gained 50c.

Worse still, if the stock trades below $5, then your option will expire worthless. There is no point exercising an option to buy stock for $5 if it can be bought more cheaply on the open market. In this case you will have made a total loss of $6 - the entire, original purchase price of the option. There is a small compensation in that you have had the use of $4 capital for a full year, which is not the case for an investor with ownership of the stock.

This is the principle of **leverage.** Options allow you to make higher returns for a smaller investment, but at the cost of much greater losses if the investment thesis does not play out.

We have looked at a Call option from the point of view of the a person buying the option. But for every buyer there must be a seller. So let's now consider the case of the person selling the call option.

Imagine that you own a share in stock XXX currently valued at $10. You decide to sell a call option for $6 giving the buyer the right to buy your stock for $5 in a year's time. What are the possible outcomes?

If the stock trades below $5 the option will not be exercised. You will be sitting on a paper loss of over $5 on the value of the stock, but to make up for it you will have pocketed a nice $6 premium and had use of that extra cash for a full year (which you may have invested in something more profitable).

If the stock trades above $5, the option will be exercised and you will have sold your stock having an original value of $10 for $11, making a 10% profit

---

[9] This discussion applies to American style call options, which are the norm. European style options may only be exercised at the expiration date, are generally traded on indices, and are of less interest to the retail investor.

and having the use of $6 for a full year in the meanwhile. How you feel about this may be tempered by events in the marketplace.

If stock XXX is currently trading at $6 a share, you will feel especially pleased with yourself - you've turned a potential $4 paper loss into a real $1 profit! But what if stock XXX is trading at $20? You have turned down a $10 (100%) juicy profit for a measly $1 return. Not so good.

If you own a stock, selling a call option is a conservative way to lock in some gain, at the risk of losing out if the stock price appreciates significantly. A call sold against stock which you already own is referred to as a **Covered Call**.

It is also possible to sell a call option when you do not own the stock. This is a **Naked Call**. If the stock appreciates significantly you will have to buy this stock in the market place to meet the call. This is a very risky process. The stock may be trading at many times its original value, but whatever the new price you will be forced to pay it in order to satisfy the call. This falls under the category of speculation rather than investing.

Put Options

Whereas a call option gives the owner the right to buy a stock, a **Put Option** gives the owner the right to sell a stock.

Consider that you own stock XXX with a value of $10 per share. You are generally optimistic about its prospects, but are concerned that if things don't work out as planned it may depreciate in value significantly. You could buy a put option dated one year hence at an $8 strike price. That would give you the right to sell the stock at any time during the next year, so that if the stock fell to $3, you could still sell it for $8 - happy days. But there is a downside. If it costs you $1 to buy the put option, and the stock does not depreciate, you have made a 10% loss on the stock already without doing anything. And even if the stock does fall below $8, you have effectively sold it for $7, when you take into account the price paid for the put.

You don't need to own a stock in order to purchase a put. If you feel that a stock is overvalued you could buy a put to sell for $8, hoping to pick up the stock for $4 and sell it at a profit sometime before the expiry date.

Some investors use puts as hedges - often buying puts on a stock index in order to set up a general hedge on a portfolio. As we discussed earlier, this is not a strategy favoured by the great investors.

Now let's look at the transaction from the other side. You do not own stock XXX, but decide that it is undervalued at $10 per share, and will probably rise in value. So you sell a put with a strike price of $8 for a $1 premium.

This is a notion that sometimes confuses novice investors. How can you sell something when you did not own anything in the first place? What you are effectively selling is insurance[10]. And to sell insurance you do not need to own anything. You just need to have the capacity to take on risk.

Let's explore two scenarios. What if you are right and the stock maintains a value of over $8 for the life of the put? Nothing happens. You have collected a juicy $1 premium and you keep it and move on. Just as the insurance company keeps your premium when they don't have to pay out a claim.

But what if the stock falls to $6? In this case you are obliged to buy the stock for $8. Not a happy outcome, but there are two mitigating factors. Firstly the stock only really cost you $7, because you have already booked a $1 premium. Secondly, you still have the stock and it may well appreciate in future to a price well above your equivalent $7 purchase price, allowing you to eventually book a nice profit. Of course, as with all investments, the business could falter and you could lose the whole $7. But that is true of any investment in stocks.

In an ordinary trading account, you broker will require you to hold cash to cover any put options that you sell. But if you have a margin account with sufficient collateral, you will be allowed to sell puts without holding cash to cover them. A put sold without cash cover is known as a **Naked Put**. Naked puts are risky, as you may be forced to raise cash, or trade in overdraft, in the event that the put is exercised. But a naked put is less risky than a naked call, as the maximum loss is defined by the strike price, whereas the liability for a naked call has no upper limit.

More About Options

Having covered the basic principles of how options work, let's delve into a little more detail.

Let's say that there is a stock trading at $10, and you wish to purchase a call option with a strike price of $6 and an expiration date three months hence. Let's say that you are charged $5 for the call option. If you exercise the option, the total price that you will pay is $11. This is $1 more than you would pay if you bought the stock today. This additional premium is called **Time Value**.

Time Value is the additional amount an option purchaser pays for the privilege of delaying their purchase of the stock.

The price paid for an option is generally referred to as the **Premium**.

You can think of the call option premium (price) of $5 as being made up of two components. $4 accounts for the market price of the stock (being the difference between the strike price of $6 and the current market price of $10). This is known as **Intrinsic Value**. So the option premium of $5 is made up of $4 in intrinsic valuc and $1 of timc valuc.

[10] From a practical perspective, selling options can be thought of as selling insurance. But from a legal perspective, this is not the case.

Let's consider another case. What if you are very optimistic about a stock trading at $10? In fact you are so sure that it will be trading at $15 within three months that you decide to buy a call option with a strike price of $12.

If this option were to expire tomorrow, it would be worthless. It has no intrinsic value, only time value. An option that would expire worthless at the current market price is referred to as an **Out of the Money** option (**OTM**).

Call options with a strike price above the current market price and put options with a strike price below the current market price are out of the money options.

Options that could be exercised for profit at the current market price - put options with a strike price above the current market price, or call options with a strike price below the current market price - are referred to as **In the Money** options (**ITM**).

An option with a strike price that is the same as the current market price is referred to as an **At the Money** option (**ATM**).

Only in the money options have intrinsic value. Out of the money options have only time value.

We can define intrinsic value (IV) arithmetically as:

IV = Market Price - Strike price (for a call)

or

IV = Strike price - Market Price (for a put)

And we can define time value (TV) as:

TV = Option Price - IV

If you wish to use options effectively, you must learn how to use time value. Investors who buy call options with a view to purchasing a stock will always be paying more than the current market value, because they must pay for the time value. Investors who buy put options, and subsequently exercise them to sell a declining stock, will always receive less than the current value of the stock because they must pay for the time value. And if the stock holds its value and the put expires worthless, then the investor has paid for the time value for no monetary return.

Investors who sell call options will always receive more than the current market value if the option is eventually exercised, because they have gained the benefit of the time value. And if the option is not exercised, they simply keep the premium. Investors who sell put options will always pay less than the current market value of the stock if the option is exercised, because they have the benefit of the time value. And if not they keep the premium.

Another important fact you need to know about options is that they are always sold in blocks of 100. So if you purchase a $1 call option on a $10 stock, you will need to pay $100 for the purchase and if you exercise the option you will be required to pay $1,000 for 100 shares.

This is fine if you are dealing with stocks priced at $10, but with some stocks on the market priced at $1,000 or more, dealing in lots of $100,000 may be a little intimidating for the novice investor!

Often, you may read about investors that have made a killing buying options. They may buy a call option for $1 on $10 stock. Then, following an unexpectedly good earnings report, the stock soars to $20. The value of the option now becomes $10 - they have made a 10 times return on their investment in a very short time period! That's five times better than the people who owned the stock, who only doubled their money!

Sounds great doesn't it? The only problem is that for every time that happens, there will be far more instances when the stock price falls or appreciates by only a small amount, and that results in a loss of 100% of the premium. The market is not stupid. Options are priced for the market makers and just as you can have a good day at the races once in a while, if you keep turning up at the track, your bank account will surely dwindle, and the bookmakers will keep returning to their mansions in the country.

So forget about making the big deal or the quick killing in the options market. These high-return trades made at the margin are gambles. Buffett doesn't try for them, and Lynch avoided them like the plague. The way to make money in the stock market is to learn from the great investors.

There is a smart way for you to use the options market, and turn it to your advantage.

Imagine that you have performed your analysis of stock XXX and you are ready and willing to pay $10 for the stock. Instead of buying the stock for $10, sell a $9 put for $1.

There are two outcomes possible. The stock stays above $9 and you keep the $1 premium. Or the stock drifts below $9 let's say to $7. You are now obliged to take the stock at $9. If you take into account the $1 premium you have effectively paid $8 for a $7 stock. But that stock is a stock for which you were prepared to pay $10. And if your investment thesis plays out, it will grow in your portfolio and make a healthy profit one day.

This almost seems like a no lose proposition. But things can go badly wrong. If you are right about the stock and it suddenly sails up to $30, you have missed the boat and the $1 premium that you have received seems scant compensation.

Smart investors use options judiciously. If you like a stock, buy it. But maybe sell a few put options on the side. If you are required to take the stock, it's not such a bad thing, because you were building a holding of that stock in your portfolio anyway. (But take note that you have no way of knowing whether a put option will be exercised. That is why should should buy your main allocation of the stock, and treat the option trade as supplemental to your strategy. Think of it as creating a little extra juice around the edges.)

If you have a holding that has become overweight, sell a few call options. Not enough to take away your entire holding, but just enough to trim the position. If the call options expire with the stock above the strike price, sell some more call options. Keep doing this until the stock is called away. By proceeding in this fashion you can collect useful premiums and you are guaranteed to sell the stock above the current market price when it is eventually called away.

Selling put options is a favoured strategy of Warren Buffett.

In fact, selling put options can seem like a fantastic way to keep collecting 'money for nothing'. When the market is rising, every time you sell a put option you keep collecting premium and don't have to do anything. But there is a major danger here for small investors.

For small accounts, brokers will expect you to hold cash to cover sold put options, to ensure that you can afford to pay for the shares if you are obliged to take them. There is no real danger here.

But for more significant accounts, the broker will offer you 'margin'. This allows you to buy stocks using borrowed money, or to sell put options using your existing stock holdings as collateral. If you get addicted to selling put options for income and the market has a significant fall, you can suddenly find that you are being asked to take large amounts of stock with no money to pay for them.

This situation then becomes exacerbated as the stocks that you hold as collateral are now also falling in value and you find yourself having to make forced sales at the worst possible time in order to raise cash. Or even worse, your broker may sell stock indiscriminately in order to bring your account back within margin requirements.

This occurrence can have a devastating effect upon a portfolio, and can wipe out all of the profits made painstakingly over the years together with a large proportion of the starting capital.

For this reason, many investors avoid options altogether. Not because they don't understand how they can be used to add a little extra return by selling time value, but because they are afraid to become seduced into over-selling puts and courting disaster.

Summary

Derivatives are devices that enable you to carry out financial transactions based upon the price of an underlying asset.

Futures and Shorts can be toxic investments and should be avoided by the small investor.

Options have a use in a cautiously managed portfolio if you use them as an attempt to buy stock that you like cheaply, or to trim a holding that has become overweight.

Do not sell put options unless you are fully prepared to take the stock, and **in no circumstances** should you oversell put options.

You will not get a better lesson in the dangers on selling puts, than to read the following message that was posted to a Motley Fool message board by user 2001Cobra on 25th January 2013.

> ***Subject: Don't be like me...***
>
> *I don't know where to begin. I don't even know what to say. I just know I need to write this down to get my feelings on paper. I am in a pretty dark place right now. A dark place that is my own doing. I have to accept that this situation was caused by my ignorance, pride, and a lack of respect for the market forces in general…*
>
> *I thought I was so smart last year. I bought calls, sold PUTs, and was making a lot of extra money on Apple. Extra money that felt like it was 'free'. At one point, every PUT I sold made me money. I was plus $16 thousand dollars last year...*
>
> *I was lucky to find this board. At one point last year, I had 8 PUTs that I had sold. I was sure no way Apple would drop down past $640, $600, $580, $560, and $550. Those were just a few of the PUTS I had written for Jan '13. Thanks to JS, Huibs, and a few others I was able to start off loading those PUTs because I had insane amounts of leverage should anything go wrong for my portfolio size...*
>
> *But, I kept two. I just KNEW no way AAPLE would be below these strike prices going into the largest and best Quarter with a brand new Iphone 5 and Ipad Mini. I didn't care that even holding 2 PUTs were probably too much for my portfolio size. I was POSITIVE AAPL would kill it and I would again be making 'free' money..*

But then, AAPL started dropping. I thought this was crazy. Soon it was $650 and I started selling a few of my more risky stocks to add. Then it was $600 and I sold some more stock to add to my AAPL holdings. Then $550. I knew people were crazy and I kept adding to shares by selling off other parts of my portfolio. Then AAPL was sub $500 and I added some more. I didn't care that I was overweight because AAPL would announce fantastic earnings and we would be off on a rocket ship back to $700/share...

What's AAPL at right now? $440. Because I kept the Jan $610 which has since been rolled down to a March $585 and the April $600 I am a touch over $30K in the red. What did I get when I wrote those 2 PUTs originally-- a grand total of $5K...

But, that's not the worst of it. The worst of it has been the shares I added on the way down by selling off other parts of my portfolio. I am now down > $100K in less than 3 months. I own almost nothing but AAPL stock and I will need to sell the rest of my entire portfolio just to buy back 1 PUT. All I have left is SBUX, WFM, ATVI, IDCC, WPRT, and a few stocks here or there with only a couple thousand in them. That's all I can afford to do unless I start selling AAPL shares at $440…

I have destroyed my net worth. 10+ years of saving and scrimping and adding to new stocks over time erased in 3 months...

The worst part, I can't even really explain it. AAPL has $130B+ in cash, just announced record earnings, and the market is punishing them. The PE after you back out the cash is < 7 for the highest earnings EVER for a none Oil Company. But, it doesn't matter. I can argue till I'm blue in the face about how unfair it is that AAPL is being valued less than MSFT or that AMZN has only earning $5B in their lifetime but goes for a PE that is in the *hundreds. The only thing that matters is AAPLE sold off about 38% and I got slaughtered due to my recklessness. I over allocated and sold PUTs I can no longer afford. I did have the cash to cover them at one point until I started selling those stocks to add to my AAPL holdings because it was just to "cheap"...*

This is pretty much the worst thing I have ever done and my biggest mistake ever. I haven't even told my wife that I erased our retirement funds and that we can no longer afford the vacation to Hawaii like we had been planning. We just can't go. I have to tell her we can't go because I lost > $100K by doubling, tripling my AAPL holdings all the way down while holding onto 2 extremely underwater PUTs that I still need to figure out what to do with...

I don't know what the future holds for me and my family. Maybe I'll be divorced in 6 months because of what I did. I really don't know. I feel ashamed. I feel, hopeless I guess. I just needed to write this down. I hope it saves 1 person from doing what I did...

The sad part is, I am a pretty smart guy. I Have two Doctorate degrees, am board certified in Sports Medicine, and have published research articles in respected Journals. But, none of that matters here. Here, I am just a stupid investor that didn't heed warnings and has no place in the stock market anymore...

This will be my last post. Then, I will be disappearing for a while. I canceled my MF Options subscription and may cancel the one here. I am not sure yet. I just know I need to spend the next few weeks and months salvaging what I can from my relationships and from what I have left in my brokerage account...

Cobra--AAPL at $437 and with no end in sight. Management isn't even trying to defend the stock. Bought a paltry $2B last Qrt in buybacks. Obviously, not buying today to support the price

Maybe I'll see you guys later. Maybe not. Good luck and good fortune…

Investing Style

I Am What I Am

At the outset of this book I set out to show you how to make considerable sums of money in the stock market by following the methods of the world's greatest investors.

You may say, why bother? Why don't I just look at Warren Buffett's portfolio and copy that?

Many have tried, but with limited success.

In the first place, Buffett doesn't tell you what he does in real time - you would have to rely on quarterly reports which are always out of date. In the second place, Buffett's capital pool is so large that he has to operate within far more constraints than the average retail investor. And finally, Buffett has investment opportunities open to him that simply don't exist for the small investor. Not only does he have access to specialist financial products created by the investment banks for exclusive use by their closest clients, but he can negotiate his own deals - and frequently does - as when he bailed out Bank of America during the financial crisis.

All of this makes it impossible to copy exactly what Buffett does. But even if you could track his trading accurately, it would still be a bad idea.

One of the things that you learn by studying the great investors, is that they are all unique. They do not follow a method that relies on any strict set of rules. Instead they develop a style that suits their own abilities and personality.

Buffett is famously reticent to invest in technology stocks. Some of the most fantastic returns in the stock market over the last few decades have come from the technology sector. Yet Buffett has still managed to trounce the market while avoiding technology almost completely. (He took a major stake in Apple but only after it had grown into a huge mature business).

Buffett likes to invest in companies that he feels comfortable with and can understand. He refers to this as his **circle of competence**.

The best way to emulate Buffett is not to blindly follow his stock picks, but to follow his approach. You need to find your own circle of competence.

Buffett is attracted to high quality businesses with strong brands and competent management. He is not so fond of high growth companies. Lynch, on the other hand, loves high growth businesses. But Lynch also likes to balance out his portfolio with stable established businesses - stalwarts in Lynch-speak. He also likes to invest in cyclicals (such as automotive companies) and turn around stories.

Whereas Buffett likes to own a high quality business and sit tight. Lynch likes to hold his growth stocks but rotate his stalwarts and cyclicals. Don't get me wrong, Lynch is not a 'day trader' but he trims or adds to his core holdings as the P/E fluctuates between its historic highs and lows.

Neither of these approaches is 'right' or 'wrong'. Buffett's approach is right for Buffett, and Lynch's approach is right for Lynch.

The approaches taken by all of the great investors, such as Shelby Davis, Philip Fisher or Tom Gayner, are all unique and have matured with experience. They all have their own style and their own circle of competence.

In Guy Thomas's 'Free Capital' all of the investors studied admitted to not being very successful at first, but by persisting, they found their own style and started to make money. Buffett often talks about how his style has developed and improved - greatly influenced by his close friend and business partner Charlie Munger.

In order to become a great investor you have to be persistent, patient and develop a style of your own.

As you become familiar with businesses through reading annual reports, listening to conference calls, and following their progress quarter by quarter, year by year, you will find that you are drawn to some companies and feel less comfortable with others.

One investor may be happy with a portfolio of ten high growth companies, getting a ten-bagger, a five-bagger and eight duds over the first few years to get an increase of 50%. Another investor may have ten sturdy and reliable businesses growing modestly to achieve the same result.

You will not find your style straight away.

We think we know ourselves, but sometimes we find that when push comes to shove we can be cautious where we expected to be brave. Or we may become reckless when we expected to be conservative.

The most important thing to remember about taking your first steps as an investor is that it is OK to make mistakes. It is meant to be a learning process. The one thing that you must do is make sure that you adapt and learn.

One of the most important 'investments' that you make is the investment in time that it takes to find your own personal modus operandi.

Einstein defined insanity as 'doing the same thing over and over again and expecting different results'.

Don't be insane.

Selling

One of the most popular questions asked by novice investors is, 'when do I sell?'.

You have bought your first position, and hey presto! It's up by twenty percent.

What could be better than the instant gratification of pocketing the moolah and patting yourself on the back? As the talking heads on the media never tire of saying, 'it's never bad to take a little profit off the table'.

On the other hand, it could be that you have made your first investment, and disaster strikes - it's down twenty percent. Better sell quickly, before it falls further. Again, you hear the talking heads speaking into your ear, 'where's your sell discipline?'.

It seems that whatever the position, there is a constant pressure to sell. But if you cave in to this pressure, you are almost certain to fail as an investor. The lesson from the great investors is clear, the best returns come from long-term buy and hold investing.

Fidelity investments carried out a survey to determine which of their investors had the highest performance. The survey ran from 2003 to 2013. The results where clear - the best performing investors were either dead or inactive.

The Motley Fool stock advisor service did an analysis of their performance in May 2014, and found that even though they had done very well against the market, if they had never issued a Sell recommendation they would have improved their performance by a further fifty one percent[11].

The greatest investor of them all, Buffett, says, 'When we own portions of outstanding businesses with outstanding managements, our favourite holding period is forever'.

The message is clear then - sell at your peril.

There are three occasions when you should let a stock go:

- When the reason you bought the stock no longer applies and no better story has emerged to take its place
- When it becomes such a huge portion of your portfolio that it should be trimmed for risk management reasons
- When you need the money for something more important - such as children's college fees or buying a house

The second and third reasons require little explanation. A sale in those circumstances is a mandatory event.

---

[11] The service achieved a gain of 210% as against 51% for the S&P500, which would have improved to a 261% gain if they had not made their sell recommendations.

The first, requires a little more thought - a lot depends on 'the reason you bought the stock'.

Perhaps you think that the reason you bought the stock was that you thought it would go up, but now you think it might go down. So - Sell! Sell! Sell!

This is the sort of thinking that gets you into deep trouble.

If you bought the stock because the company was about to release a drug that could cure cancer, but now it transpires that tests show it has no clinical effect, and it has been banned by the Food and Drug Administration, then it can safely be said that the reason you bought the stock no longer applies.

There is a big difference between a change on a whim and a genuine change to a deeply thought out investment thesis.

Peter Lynch allocated about thirty percent of his portfolio to companies he categorized as stalwarts - big companies that are unlikely to fail. He would track their current P/E against their historical P/E and if it got too rich, he would sell the stock - or perhaps a portion of his holding. And then he would replace it with a stock tracking at the lower range of its historical P/E. To some, this may seem like day trading. But it is actually a carefully thought out thesis, followed with a rigorous adherence to his investment strategy. And for stalwarts with slow moving prices, these changes may take place over many months or years. The selling rule most definitely applies here. The reason to buy the stock was that it was a stalwart trading at a low P/E - when the stalwart is trading at a high P/E the reason Lynch bought the stock no longer applies.

It is important to note that Lynch treated his stalwarts like this - not his growth companies.

If you have made an investment in a company which you see as having great growth over the next decade, one or two dodgy quarters do not meet the criteria of a change in thesis, and should not be used a valid reason to sell the stock.

When prices fluctuate wildly, you may find it difficult to hold your nerve. Remember that the most important asset of a great investor is a good temperament.

Two reasons are often given for selling stocks, which are potentially dangerous.

(1) Sell if you find a better place to put your money

Investors are always wanting to 'do something'. If a stock has been immobile for a while and you have just read a convincing pitch on a new and upcoming company, the temptation to sell the stock you hold and buy the shiny new prospect becomes irresistible. No sooner have you made the switch, than the previously immobile stock will suddenly spurt ahead, and your new holding will crash.

(2) Imagine that a mistake caused all your holdings to be sold overnight. Would you re-build your portfolio as it is now?

The inference being that you should periodically rebalance your portfolio by selling your larger holdings, and recreate your portfolio as if you were starting afresh. On the surface, this advice appears logical. But in reality, this is another way of trimming the flowers and watering the weeds.

The problem with both of these pieces of advice is that they pander to the investor's penchant for finding something to do - which nearly always leads to a worse situation.

It is almost inevitable that as a novice investor you will make sales that you come to regret.

Lynch has done it. Buffett has done it - pretty much every investor does it at some time.

The quicker you learn patience the, quicker your returns will improve.

When your hand twitches over the sell button, think of Fidelity, and remember the skillful dead…

Finding Investments

Needles and Haystacks

Throughout this book we have concentrated on how to evaluate companies as investment candidates. But there are thousands of companies quoted on stock markets all over the world. Where do you start?

Companies are mentioned all the time in newspapers, television and on the internet.

As a developing investor one of the first sources of information that you may encounter are the various investment orientated business programmes such as those presented in the morning on CNBC and Bloomberg television.

These programmes tend to focus on short term news and short term stock movements - which is the antithesis of the approach that we have developed by focussing on the methods of the great investors.

Many newspapers offer investment columns, and some magazines specialize in investment matters. These may be a better source of information.

Another great way to find ideas is to follow the Lynch method - keep your eyes out whenever you take a trip or visit the shops. If you see a business that's thriving, find out if it's a publicly quoted company.

In 'Common Stocks and Uncommon Profits' Philip Fisher confesses that he was surprised to discover that most of his best investment ideas came from studying the ideas of other investment professionals.

There are investment websites where you can read articles and communicate with other users to discuss investment issues and pick up stock ideas.

There are also advisory services that will provide you with 'stock picks', as suggestions for investment.

The main advantage of the coverage found in newspapers - and to a greater degree, in investment magazines - is that much of the analysis has been done for you. The company may have been valued on a P/E or PEG basis, and an investment thesis has already been sketched out. (This does not relieve you of the ultimate responsibility of carrying out your own analysis - it relieves you of the burden of carrying it out unnecessarily on an unpromising business.)

If you subscribe to an investment advisory service, you will get a deeper analysis and a more detailed investment story.

All of these methods and services provide a great way to filter out the noise and unearth those companies with good investment characteristics.

If you decide that subscribing to an investment advisory service is a good idea, make sure that it has a philosophy compatible with your own. If you are following a long-term buy and hold strategy in the mould of Buffett, Lynch and Davis, there is not a lot of value to be gained from a service recommending short term option trades. Only use a service with a rock solid reputation, with published results that you can compare against the S&P500 (or a suitable relevant index).

Once subscribed to a service, never buy a stock solely on recommendation. A recommendation is the start of your work, not the end of it.

Rushing into a stock on a whim because it was just recommended with a particularly convincing pitch in a newsletter, is one of the most common mistakes made by the novice investor.

Buffett said this, 'I could improve your ultimate financial welfare by giving you a ticket with only twenty slots in it so that you had twenty punches - representing all the investments that you got to make in a lifetime. And once you'd punched through the card, you couldn't make any more investments at all. Under those rules, you'd really think carefully about what you did, and you'd be forced to load up on what you'd really thought about. So you'd do so much better'.

If you subscribe to a service making monthly stock picks, remember that the service is under an obligation to find a stock every month, whether or not a good investment candidate is available. Rather than look to the newly recommended stock for your first idea, look for the stocks that have been highlighted as the long-term favourites of the service.

Wherever you look for your ideas, it is important to remain open-minded and ready to seek out new ideas from many sources.

Newsletters, magazines and stock services are not there to do your thinking for you, they are there to provide a necessary filter. They enable you to get to work on a short-list, instead of trying to work your way through thousands of companies.

Once a candidate stock has passed through the filter, wipe the slate clean, and forget what came from the newsletter or service. Go to the investors relations section of the company's web site and read the latest filings and releases - the last annual report, the last few quarterly reports, recent press releases, and any investor presentations. Follow the process we have outlined in this book, and form a new opinion of the business, the only opinion that matters - your own.

Summary

At the start of this book I made the suggestion that it is possible for the average person, without special effort, to become wealthy through investing in stocks.

To convince you of this, I gave the example of the eighteen-year-old saving $20 per week in a stock index fund — which almost certainly will accumulate in excess of $1M over a lifetime.

And I told you about Anne Scheiber — a clerk who never earned more than $4,000 per year, yet she accumulated a fortune of $22M by investing in stocks.

With those examples in mind, we set out upon our journey into the world of stock investing.

The examples I gave you had two common factors. They both had time. And they both assume a decent rate of return.

In chapter one, we addressed a fundamental question: Why stocks?

We looked at the alternatives — cash deposits, bonds, real estate — and found them all wanting. Cash barely keeps pace with inflation. Bonds, as Warren Buffett noted, are "among the most dangerous of assets" because inflation slowly destroys their purchasing power. Real estate requires enormous capital and comes with ongoing costs and headaches.

Stocks are different. When you buy a stock, you become part-owner of a real business. And throughout history, ownership of successful businesses has been the most reliable path to wealth.

We introduced the idea of compound magic. We used the example of $1,000 invested for a twenty-year-old, with the aim to provide a lump sum to withdraw at a retirement age of sixty. We postulated that an investment in a stock index fund would return 10% (the historical average). We further assumed that an accomplished investor might achieve 15% or 20%, depending on the level of skill.

The amount withdrawn at sixty for the various levels of return would be as follows:

Rate of Return	Value at Age 60
1.5% (cash)	$1,814
5% (bonds)	$7,040
10% (market average)	$45,259
15% (skilled investor)	$267,864
20% (expert investor)	$1,469,772

Grasping the significance of time and rate of return is the most important lesson that you can learn from this book. Even a small increase in percentage return can make a huge difference to an amount invested over time.

Once grasped, the conclusions are obvious. Put away as much as you can as early as you can. And having done that, do whatever you can to increase the rate of return.

How can we find a way to increase our returns? If you wanted to become a great golfer, what would you do? Would you study the physics of the golf swing? Or would you watch the great golfers and then get out on the course and practice?

There are those who study learned papers on modern portfolio theory in order to improve their investment returns. But the approach we have taken together has been instead to follow the masters and attempt to emulate them. An approach vindicated in part by the fact that, upon examination, it seems that successful investors tend to be very dismissive of the academic theorists.

In chapter two, we noted that successful investors fly in the face of conventional wisdom. Most financial advisors suggest a diversified portfolio with a mixture of stocks and bonds. But the successful investors tend to have a concentrated portfolio consisting only of stocks.

Bonds should be avoided. The evidence is clear: to make superior investment returns, your portfolio should be concentrated in stocks.

The number of stocks will vary according to personal style—but as a rough guide, somewhere around ten would be the minimum, with around fifteen being the average. Some investors prefer more concentration with as few as six stocks, while others may hold up to fifty if they have the time to follow that many businesses properly.

We also looked at investing style and concluded that the best investors employ a long-term buy-and-hold strategy and do not try to "time the market." Over time, long-term returns tend to come from a few big winners that will emerge as your portfolio develops.

By the time we reached the third chapter, we had enough information to form our investment strategy—the magic plan:

The Magic Plan:

- **Don't get into debt**—especially credit card debt.
- **Follow Buffett's advice:** "Do not save what is left after spending, but spend what is left after saving."
- **Keep an Emergency Fund** - this book is about money that you can afford to set aside over the long term.
- **Build an investment portfolio** by creating a collection of stocks—preferably in a tax-sheltered account.

- **Start simple.** Begin with index funds if you're just starting out, then transition to individual stocks as your knowledge grows.
- **Keep learning.** The more you understand about businesses and investing, the better your returns will be.

With our plan in mind, we set out to discover how we should select the best companies for investment.

The next chapter was very short, but with a very important message. **To own a stock is to own a part share in a business.** This attitude is ingrained into the very soul of the great investors like Buffett and Lynch. If there is any one secret to achieving great investment returns, then this is it.

As a corollary of this insight, in chapter five we spent some time looking at the characteristics of successful businesses. The most important attribute that a business can possess is a competitive advantage.

Competitive advantage can come from:

- Disruptive Innovation
- Sustaining Innovation
- Financial Engineering
- Brilliant Execution
- Ownership of valuable intellectual property (such as a patent, copyright, or brand)

The other important business qualities that can elevate a business above its competitors are:

- Good Management
- Strong Balance Sheet
- Growing Revenues
- Growing Profitability
- Strong Cash Flow
- Good Return on Capital
- Strong Corporate Culture
- Large Total Addressable Market
- Reinvestment Potential
- Low Capital Requirement
- Provide a Good Personal Experience
- Low Profile Industry
- Special Circumstances
- Reasonable Share Price

Business qualities address the first part of our process. But it is equally important for us to ask, "Where is the business going?", "Does the story make sense?"

The story—or the investment thesis, as it is generally called—goes to the heart of the investment process. Investing is forward-looking. Without an investment thesis, there is no investment.

Having established our modus operandi in chapters one to six, in the next stage of our journey we started to build up our toolkit of investor essentials.

In chapter seven, "Understanding the Numbers," we found out how we should interpret a company's financial statements.

Novices often find financial statements intimidating—but in reality, there is nothing to fear. Once we become accustomed to the layout and the jargon, interpreting the financial statements largely comes down to looking for the obvious and using common sense.

The income statement tells us whether the business is making money. The balance sheet paints a picture of a company's resources. And the cash flow statement shows us where the money comes from—and also where it goes.

Next, we looked at the various ways to value a business. We started with a common-sense approach—"How much is this business worth to me, given the investment alternatives available?" And then we moved on to look at the valuation methods generally used by the market professionals—discounted cash flow (DCF), the price-to-earnings ratio (P/E), the price-to-sales ratio, and the price-to-book value ratio.

We looked at the limitations of DCF and noted that successful investors shy away from it. Lynch favored the P/E ratio as the way to value businesses—particularly in its extended form, the PEG ratio. The PEG ratio is calculated by dividing the P/E by the growth percentage.

There is no single valuation method that can be applied to all businesses. The best approach is to use common sense to identify the most appropriate metric and form a view as to how the business is likely to develop into the future. Successful investors are wary of any overly precise method of valuation—they make simple calculations based on simple assumptions. Business judgment trumps mathematical complexity every time.

The next thing we covered was risk.

To an investor, risk may be defined as the possibility that an investment will result in a permanent, significant loss of capital.

There are two types of risk. Major risk occurs when there is a possibility of a single event or failure that could threaten the entire investment. Cumulative risk arises through an accumulation of minor issues which, although not serious in themselves, may combine to overwhelm a business.

All risks are not equal. Every investment has an element of risk. It is down to the business judgment of the investor to decide whether the level of risk in an investment is acceptable.

There are no extra prizes for heroism in investing. Or as Buffett puts it, "Overall we've done better by avoiding dragons than by slaying them."

We also looked at Tesla and Westport Innovations—two companies with compelling stories but very different outcomes. Tesla, led by visionary Elon Musk, went on to become one of the most valuable companies in the world. Westport, despite having what seemed like a more sensible business case, struggled and never recovered. The lesson? Sometimes the "riskier" bet on exceptional leadership and disruptive innovation pays off far better than the "safer" bet on simple economics.

Investing is more art than science, and in the next chapter we warmed to that theme by considering the importance of getting to know the businesses that you invest in on a personal level.

Becoming acquainted with the culture, attitudes, and values of a business is just as important, if not more so, than an in-depth grasp of the financials. Getting to know the passions, prejudices, and motivations of the CEO is key to developing a deep understanding of a business. The first indication of whether headwinds or tailwinds lie ahead can often be found in the mannerisms of the CEO.

Next, we took a whirlwind tour of derivatives. Successful investors use options and leverage sparingly, if at all. In certain limited circumstances, there may be some advantage to selling puts in order to buy stock more cheaply or selling calls in order to sell stock at a better price. But this must be offset against the danger posed by options. Overuse of options can prove catastrophic to an investment portfolio.

We considered how an individual's personality affects our investing approach. Every investor is different. There are many similarities between the investment styles of Buffett, Lynch, and Davis. But there are also significant differences.

The purpose of this book has been to weave a common thread amongst the style of the greats, to find a template that we can use as a guide to the best investment approach.

But each one of us is an individual, and the investment style that suits you may not be the one to suit me. In fact, one of the major discoveries of our study of great investors is that it is important to find a personal style and not try to blindly copy the style of another.

Yes, there are common themes:

- Invest in businesses, not stock tickers
- Keep a concentrated portfolio based around common stocks
- Get to know your businesses well
- Be patient with your investments and keep a calm temperament
- Avoid overuse of leverage

But there is also great scope for divergence. Do you prefer growth stocks or dividend payers? Do you like and understand technology, or would you prefer established industries that are not prone to disruption?

There are many questions like these that can only be addressed by you alone. It takes time to learn about yourself and to find your style. Learn as you go and let your style develop.

Next we considered the vexed question of selling.

There are three reasons to sell a stock:

- When the reason you bought the stock no longer applies and no better story has emerged to take its place
- When it becomes such a huge portion of your portfolio that it should be trimmed for risk management reasons
- When you need the money for something more important—such as children's college fees or buying a house

The main mistake made by novice investors is to misinterpret "the reason you bought the stock no longer applies."

Action always feels better than inaction—and we find it easy to convince ourselves that some minor hiccup amounts to sufficient reason to sell a business that we own. Regret nearly always follows, if not sooner, then later.

Be disciplined, hold your nerve, and consider very carefully before you sell a stock. There will be times when a sale is the right decision. Sometimes it is necessary to harvest a capital loss for tax reasons. That would be a good time to sell a business for which the investment thesis is well and truly broken. But before making the final decision—think of Fidelity and the skillful dead.

And so we come to the end of our little reprise. What are the most important things we have learned?

- **Stocks are the superior vehicle for building long-term wealth**
- Time and rate of return are fundamental
- The best rates of return are to be found in common stocks
- Own businesses, not stock tickers
- A calm temperament is the most important quality an investor can have
- Concentrate your portfolio in stocks—bonds have no place in a wealth-building portfolio

That is how I might phrase it.

But who does the greatest investor of all turn to for advice?

Warren Buffett's great friend and partner, Charlie Munger, expressed the secret of successful investing with characteristic pith. And I cannot think of any better advice with which to end this book.

"Find great companies and sit on your ass."

Appendix

Essential Additional Reading

One up on Wall Street - Peter Lynch

The Outsiders - William Thorndike

The Innovators Dilemma - Clayton Christensen

The Essays of Warren Buffett: Lessons for Corporate America - Selected and arranged by Lawrence A. Cunningham

The Snowball - Alice Schroeder

The Davis Dynasty - John Rothschild

Common Stocks and Uncommon Profits - Philip Fisher

Glossary

10Q - Quarterly Financial Report filed with the S.E.C. in the U.S.A.

10K - Annual Financial Report filed with the S.E.C. in the U.S.A.

8K - Report on a significant event filed with the S.E.C. in the U.S.A.

Accrual - An amount charged against profit for an un-invoiced revenue or expense.

Accruals Principle - The principle that income and expenditure should be recorded in the period to which it relates - regardless of when cash flows occur.

Acid Test - A financial ratio measuring a company's liquidity. It is measured by taking current assets less inventory divided by current liabilities.

Acquisition - When one business buys the entire assets of another business, it is referred to as an acquisition.

Adjusted Earnings - Company's are required to produce accounts in accordance with generally accepted accounting principles (GAAP). Sometimes management produces alternative, adjusted accounts. The earnings reported on these adjusted accounts are the adjusted earnings.

Amortization - The diminution in value of an intangible asset - equivalent to the depreciation of a fixed asset.

Ask Price - The lowest price that a seller of a security is prepared to accept.

Asset - An item that has value, such as cash, a debt, a building, or intellectual property.

Bagger - Used in conjunction with a number to express the gain made on an investment. A two bagger returns double the original investment. A ten bagger returns ten times the original investment.

Balance Sheet - A financial report showing a company's assets and liabilities.

Berkshire Hathaway - An American multi-national company, run by CEO Warren Buffett.

Beta - The sensitivity of a stock price to a movement in prices in the general market..

Bezos, Jeff - CEO of Amazon.

Bid Price - The highest price that a buyer of a security is prepared to accept.

Bid Ask Spread - The difference between the bid price and the ask price of a security.

Blue Chip - Used as an adjective to denote a very high quality company.

Bond, Government - A security that pays interest, issued by a government.

Bond, Corporate - A security that pays interest, issued by a corporation.

Book Value - The value of assets less liabilities for a company as reported in the company's published accounts.

Brand - The value of a product name that has been established by its public reputation.

Branson, Richard - CEO of Virgin.

Broker - A company that provides a service for buying and selling securities.

Buffett, Warren - CEO of Berkshire Hathaway, widely regarded as the world's greatest investor.

Building Society - A UK institution owned by its members that provides the same services as a bank.

Buy and Hold - A style of investing whereby securities are held for long periods of time.

Call - An option to buy a security.

Capital Allocation - The process of deciding how to deploy available capital. The capital of a business can be deployed in many ways such as paying dividends, buying back shares, making an acquisition, or reinvesting in the business.

Capital Light - A business that does not require large amounts of capital to be invested before it can make a profit. A recruitment agency is capital light, whereas an aircraft company is not.

Cash Burn - The rate at which cash is depleted when a young growing company builds a business, before profitable trading starts.

Cash Flow - The levels of cash flowing into and out of a business.

Cash Flow from Operations - The amount of cash generated from core business operations, excluding investing and financing activities.

CEO - Chief Executive Officer, the managing director in overall charge of a business.

CFO - Chief Financial Officer, the financial director in overall charge of the finances of a business reporting to the CEO.

Christensen, Clayton - Professor of Business Administration at the Harvard Business School, Author of, 'The Innovator's Dilemma'.

Circle of Competence - Warren Buffett's description of those areas that he understands to the extent that he is willing to invest in companies operating in those areas.

Comparative Figure - The figures on a financial report that relate to the same period in the previous financial year - used for comparison purposes.

Competitive Advantage - Those attributes or qualities that a business has that give it a superior position relative to its peers.

Compounding - The process of accumulation that occurs over time. Because the base capital increases every year, a steady percentage return will generate ever increasing amounts of income (10% of 100 is 10, but for the following year 10% of 110 is 11, ...)

Compound Interest - The amount of interest generated by a compounding investment (see above).

COO - Chief Operating Officer, the director in overall charge of the operations of a business reporting to the CEO.

Covered Call - A sold call which is underpinned by an owned investment in the same security.

Contract for Difference - a contract between two parties such that the seller will pay to the buyer the difference between the current value of an asset and its value at contract time.

Cost of Capital - the rate of return that a business must pay in order to access funds.

Cost of Debt - the rate of return that a business must pay in order to secure debt financing.

Cost of Equity - the rate of return that a business must pay in order to secure equity financing (i.e. by issuing shares).

CR - see credit.

Credit - (1) a period of time allowed by one party to another before settling an obligation (2) an entry made into the right hand side of an accounting ledger which relates to an income or a liability.

Creditor - A party to which credit has been extended.

Current Assets - Cash and other assets that can be converted into cash within a relatively short period, such as short term investments, accounts receivable, or inventory.

Current Liabilities - Obligations that must be settled within one year.

Current Ratio - A measure of a company's liquidity. The ratio of current assets to current liabilities.

Davis Double Play - An increased return on an investment caused by a combination of increasing earnings with an increasing multiple.

Davis, Shelby - A renowned investor, specialising in the insurance market. He achieved average returns of over 23% over a 47 year period.

Day Trader - A person who makes very short term trades on the stock market. The opposite in style to a long-term investor.

DCF - see Discounted Cash Flow.

Debit - an entry made into the left hand side of an accounting ledger which relates to an expense or an asset.

Debtor - A party with a monetary obligation to another party. Your debtors are the people that owe you money.

Dell, Michael - Founder of Dell Computer.

Depreciation - The diminution in value over time that is recorded in the accounts for a fixed asset, such as a building or a machine.

Derivative - A financial instrument that is based upon the value of an underlying asset. Call and Put options are examples of derivatives.

Diluted Shares - The number of shares that would be in issue if all the outstanding share options of a company were exercised.

Dilutive - an adjective that describes a process that would cause an increase in the number of a company's shares, and hence a reduction in the value of each individual share.

Discounted Cash Flow - a method for valuing a business by calculating the present value of all future cash flows.

Disruptive Innovation - An innovation that transforms an industry by introducing a new product or service that renders existing offerings obsolete.

Double Entry Bookkeeping - A bookkeeping process whereby transactions are entered as debit and credit entries of matching value, thus providing an automatic control mechanism.

DR - see Debit.

Earnings - The amount of profit made by a business.

Earnings Before Taxes, Depreciation and Amortization - A commonly used measure of the core operating performance of a business.

Earnings per Share - The amount of earnings that a company makes that is attributable to a single share in the business.

EBITDA - see Earnings Before Taxes, Depreciation and Amortization.

Ells, Steve - Joint CEO of Chipotle Mexican Grill. Ells is primarily responsible for the food side of the business.

Equity - The amount that a business owes to its shareholders, which is equivalent to the net assets of a business.

ETF - See Exchange Traded Fund.

Exchange Traded Fund - a marketable security that tracks a basket of assets, such as a stock index (for example, the S&P500 or FTSE 100).

FCF - see Free Cash Flow.

Financial Engineering - The process of adding value to a company's shares by financial means (in contrast to an improvement in the business itself). Share buy backs are an example of financial engineering.

Financing Activities - Activities that a business carries out in order to raise finance or repay debt. Financing activities are shown separately on a company's cash flow statement.

Fisher, Philip - An American stock investor best known as the author of 'Common Stocks and Uncommon Profits' - widely regarded as an investment classic.

Fixed Assets - Physical assets that have long-term value, which may not be converted easily into cash, such as buildings, or machinery.

Float - The amount of cash an insurance company holds in premiums for which no claims have been paid.

Free Capital - A book by Guy Thomas.

Free Cash Flow - The amount of cash generated by the operating activities of a business, less capital expenditures. It represents the cash generating capabilities of a business taking into account the amount of cash required to maintain its capital base.

Future - A contract to purchase or sell a financial security at a fixed price at a fixed date in the future.

GAAP - see Generally Accepted Accounting Principles.

Gardner, David - Co-founder of The Motley Fool stock advisory service.

Gardner, Tom - Co-founder of The Motley Fool stock advisory service.

Gates, Bill - American business magnate and founder of Microsoft.

Gayner, Tom - Highly respected chief investment officer at Markel.

Generally Accepted Accounting Principles - A set of accounting rules designed to ensure that accounts produced by different companies are directly comparable, and subscribe to widely understood standards.

Gerstner, Louis - American businessman famous for turning around IBM when it was in the depth of its troubles.

Goodwill - Goodwill is the excess amount paid over the value of a company's assets when one business acquires another.

Graham, Benjamin - Famous value investor and mentor of Warren Buffett. Author of 'Security Analysis' - published in 1934 one of the seminal texts on investing.

Growth Investor - An investor that looks for high capital growth from an investment portfolio (as opposed to high dividend payments).

Impairment - A permanent reduction in the value of an asset. Commonly used to describe a reduction in the value of intangible assets, such as goodwill.

In Search of Excellence - Seminal text on business by Tom Peters and Bob Waterman.

Income - An amount that contributes positively to a company's profit. Total income less total expenditure is the profit made by a business - its Net Income.

Income From Operations - The sum of all incomes and expenditures relating to a company's core business operations.

Income Statement - A financial statement detailing the income and expenditure of a business.

Innovators Dilemma, The - Book on disruption and innovation by Clayton Christensen.

Intangible Asset - An asset with no physical form, such as intellectual property.

Intellectual Property - an intangible asset that is the result of creativity, such as patents, copyrights.

Intrinsic Value - The value of a share option that is attributable to the price of the underlying asset. The total value of the option is a combination of intrinsic value and time value.

Inventory - Items for sale and their sub-components, also referred to as stock (UK).

Investing Activities - Activities undertaken by a business to deploy capital which is not used for operations, such as capital expenditure on equipment or investment in market securities. Shown separately on a company's cash flow statement.

Investment Thesis - The story underpinning the reason for investing in a business.

Investor - A person who purchases securities with a long-term viewpoint. The opposite in investment style to a 'trader'.

IP - see Intellectual Property.

ISA - A tax efficient savings account available to investors in the United Kingdom.

Junk Bond - A corporate bond issued by a corporation with a low credit rating.

Leverage - The use of borrowing with the aim of increasing potential returns. It will lead to increased losses if an investment doesn't work out.

Liability - An amount owed to a third party.

Liquidity - The availability of cash to a market or company.

Long-term Assets - Non-cash assets that have durable value and are not intended to be converted into cash within one year.

Long-Term Buy and Hold - Abbreviated as LTBH - A style of investing whereby investments are held over long periods. Warren Buffett is a LTBH investor. The opposite of 'trading' or 'day trading'.

Long-Term Liabilities - Obligations to third parties that do not need to be settled within one year.

LTBH - see Long-Term Buy and Hold

Lynch, Peter - Famous for managing the Fidelity Magellan Fund from 1977 to 1990 with a 29.2% average annual return. Author of the standard work on investing, 'One up on Wall Street'.

M & A - Merger and Acquisition.

Mackey, John - Proponent of 'Conscious Capitalism' as a management style, a director and co-founder of Whole Foods Market.

Malone, John - American businessman and CEO of Telecommunications Inc (TCI) and later Liberty Global. He achieved huge returns for his investors with his cash-centred approach to growth.

Margin - Borrowed money used to purchase securities.

Margin Account - An account that allows an investor to use purchased investments as security for borrowings, which may then be used to purchase further securities or engage in options transactions.

Market Capitalization - The net worth of a company's shares on a stock market.

Moat - The defence that a company has against competition from rivals.

Moran, Monty - Co-CEO of Chipotle Mexican Grill responsible for the general management of the business.

Multiple - See P / E Ratio.

Munger, Charlie - Long time business partner and friend of Warren Buffett at the helm of Berkshire Hathaway.

Musk, Elon - CEO of Tesla Motors and SpaceX.

Mutual Fund - A managed fund of investments designed to allow an individual investor to obtain a wide exposure to a selection of companies that fit into that fund's investment criteria.

Naked Call - A sold call for which no shares are held to meet the call should the option be exercised.

Naked Put - A sold put for which no cash is held to cover the assignment should the option be exercised.

Net Assets - A company's total assets less liabilities.

Net Income - A company's profit for the period.

Niederhoffer, Victor - Speculative investor and author of 'The Education of a Speculator'.

Operating Cash Flow - see Cash Flow from Operations

Operating Income - see Income from Operations

Option - A contract that gives the buyer the right, but not the obligation, to buy or sell an asset at a specific price on or before a certain date.

Outsiders, The - Book by William Thorndike on outstanding CEOs.

P/E Ratio - The ratio of a company's share price divided by its earnings per share.

PEG Ratio - The ratio of a company's P/E divided by its percentage growth.

Peters, Tom - Celebrated consultant and author of 'In Search of Excellence'.

Pink Sheets - Stocks quoted on the 'pink sheets' are over the counter securities not quoted on a major exchange. They do not need to meet minimum requirements or file with the SEC.

Prepayment - An expenditure paid in one accounting period when it relates to the following accounting period. It should be adjusted in the accounts following the accruals principle.

Price to Book Ratio - The price of one of a company's shares divided by its book value per share.

Price to Sales Ratio - The price of one of a company's shares divided by its revenues per share.

Profit - The amount of earnings retained by a company in a financial period. Equivalent to Net Income.

Profit and Loss Account - Equivalent expression for 'Income Statement' - used in the UK.

Put - An option to sell a security.

Quick Ratio - A measure of a company's liquidity, calculated by dividing current assets by current liabilities.

R&D - see Research and Development.

Rebalancing - The practice of reducing over-performing investments and reallocating the capital to underperforming investments. Otherwise known as cutting the flowers and watering the weeds.

Reinvestment Potential - The ability that a business has to easily deploy its earned income into revenue generating opportunities.

Research and Development - Activities carried out to discover and develop new products or improve and enhance existing products.

Return on Capital Employed - The amount of returns received on the capital invested. Calculated by dividing the net income of a business by its equity.

Revenue - The total sales made by a business - also referred to as turnover (UK).

Risk Free Rate - The rate of return that an investor gets by investing in risk free investments. In practice the U.S. Treasury 10 year rate is used as a benchmark.

Risk Premium - The additional rate of return achieved by investing in the general market as compared to the risk free rate.

ROCE - see Return on Capital Employed

ROTH - A tax sheltered retirement savings scheme available to investors in the U.S.A.

Salad Oil Scandal - A scandal whereby American Express issued warehouse certificates for contaminated salad oil. American Express became liable for $175M.

S&P - Standard and Poor's - An American financial services company that issues credit ratings and maintains stock market indices.

S.E.C. - Securities and Exchange Commission, the main regulatory body for the stock market in the U.S.A.

Security - A financial asset such as a share in a company or a government bond.

Seeking Alpha - An investment-based web site.

Share - A unit of ownership interest in a company or a financial asset.

Sinegal, Jim - Co-founder and former CEO of Costco.

Singleton, Henry - American engineer and businessman - founder of Teledyne Technologies.

Short - A financial transaction whereby a stock is borrowed and sold with the intention of buying it back later at a profit.

Short Seller - An investor that specializes in short transactions.

Shultz, Howard - American businessman, chairman and CEO of Starbucks.

Soros, George - Highly successful speculator in the stock market, infamous for taking on the Bank of England and winning, driving the UK out of the European exchange rate mechanism.

Speculator - A market trader that focusses on short term speculation rather than long-term investing.

Spread Bet - a bet on the price movement of a security.

Stock - (1) A type of security carrying the benefit of ownership in a company (2) Another word for inventory (UK)

Stock Based Compensation - The practice of paying employees with stock in the company as part of their remuneration package

Stock Broker - A person or organization licensed to trade in stocks

Sustaining Innovation - Improving or enhancing an existing product or service by innovative means.

TAM - see Total Addressable Market

Tangible Book Value - The book value of a company excluding intangible assets.

Thomas, Guy - Author of 'Free Capital' - a book analysing the habits of successful, amateur investors.

Thorndike, William - Author of 'The Outsiders' - a book analysing the methods of the most successful CEOs.

Time Value - The portion of the value of an option that is attributable to time (in contrast to the intrinsic value of the underlying security).

Total Addressable Market - Abbreviated as TAM - The total, worldwide value of customer spending for a product or group of products

Total Assets - The total of a company's assets excluding liabilities.

Trailing Twelve Month - Abbreviated as TTM - Used as an adjective to describe a total or financial ratio calculated by using the results of the most recent twelve months.

Treasury - Stock that a company has repurchased is described as 'held in treasury'

TTM - see Trailing Twelve Month

Turnover - Another word for sales or revenues, representing a company's total takings.

Value Investor - Someone who makes investments in situations where they perceive the real value of a company's assets to be greater than that shown in the books of account.

Volatility - a security or market index that is prone to wild swings is said of have high volatility.

Warrant - A financial instrument issued by a company that gives the owner of the warrant the right to buy the company's stock at a set price.

Warrant Revaluation - An adjustment made to a company's profits to account for a potential loss or profit realised by a change in the value of a company's warrants. As it is a non-cash adjustment it is often excluded from 'adjusted' earnings.

Waterman, Bob - Consultant and co-author of the seminal business text, 'In Search of Excellence'.

Weighted Cost of Capital - The cost of capital to a company adjusted to take account of the portion issued as debt and the portion issued as equity.

Welch, Jack - Widely acclaimed CEO of General Electric between 1981 and 2001.

Working Capital - The day to day capital required to sustain the operation of a business, represented by the value of a company's current assets less current liabilities..

Zuckerberg, Mark - CEO of Facebook.

www.ingramcontent.com/pod-product-compliance
Lightning Source LLC
LaVergne TN
LVHW050936210926
848482LV00013B/634
* 9 7 8 1 9 1 9 4 8 8 8 0 6 *